T0156562

CHOCOLATE COWS AND PURPLE CHEESE
and other tales from the homefront

CHOCOLATE COWS AND PURPLE CHEESE
and other tales from the homefront

By

Tom Hernandez

iUniverse, Inc.
New York   Bloomington

Chocolate Cows and Purple Cheese
and other tales from the homefront

iUniverse books may be ordered through booksellers or by contacting:

iUniverse
1663 Liberty Drive
Bloomington, IN 47403
www.iuniverse.com
1-800-Authors (1-800-288-4677)

Because of the dynamic nature of the Internet, any Web addresses or links contained in this book may have changed since publication and may no longer be valid. The views expressed in this work are solely those of the author and do not necessarily reflect the views of the publisher, and the publisher hereby disclaims any responsibility for them.

ISBN: 978-1-4401-3798-3 (pbk)
ISBN: 978-1-4401-3816-4 (ebk)

Printed in the United States of America

iUniverse rev. date: 4/8/2009

Introduction

Readers of my column in the Plainfield Sun newspaper sometimes ask why I called it "Homefront."

For some, the title suggests friction, war, a battleground. For others, something calmer, more familial and peaceful.

Exactly.

Every Sunday morning as I sit down at the computer to write, praying fervently that my Muse shows up before the coffee runs out, one of my daughters or my wife will often call out, "What are you writing about this week?"

"Oh, about 850 words," I reply with a practiced chuckle.

They don't laugh anymore, not even to indulge me.

Their faulty senses of humor notwithstanding, the point is that I write about life, in all of its iterations: joy, sadness, love, heartache, elation, disappointment, exhilaration, depression, certainty and doubt.

Life, dark as bright, maddening as magical, is lived on the "homefront," however you define it – relationships, home, family, parenthood, work place, faith, community, the larger world and your place in it, all of the above or none.

There is a basic rule of journalism: every story should answer the simple, yet profound question, "What does it mean?"

A simple (and simplistic) reporting of "just the facts" may fill the space in the paper, but it won't fill the reader's heart, mind or soul. Everything that is big can be made small, and vice versa.

For nearly 11 years, I've tried to show in the "Homefront" column how the most personal experiences convey universal truths while, conversely, the most world-changing events can impact individual hearts and minds.

Perhaps something in this book will make you laugh, cry, or even get angry – not necessarily because it happened to me (I hope), but because you recognize yourself in the story, no matter how big or small the topic. At least, that is my wish.

These are my thoughts, but they're about our life.

NOTE: These essays originally appeared in the Plainfield Sun newspaper between November 1998 and March 2009. They are re-published here with permission. Some have been altered slightly from their original form.

Dedication

To my wife, Kellie, who is my living, breathing blessing. You make everything better.

And to my daughters, Emma and Olivia. The moon will fall out of the sky before I stop being proud of being your dad.

Thanks

Thanks to my mother, Danna, for understanding and supporting my need to express myself all these years, even when the stories were, perhaps, a little too personal. And to my dad, Tony Hernandez, for my name, and all that has come with it. I am proud to be your "Bookie".

Thanks to my brothers, Tim and Paul for a lifetime of material – everything Mom and Dad knew about, and especially what they didn't.

Thanks to my Hernandez and Madison families – you both "adopted" me and made me feel whole, and at home.

Thanks to Pastor John Bradford, for continuing to knock on our door. The third time made a world of difference in my life.

Thanks to Dan Cassidy, my editor of 11 years, for your faith and patience every time I sent yet another last-second revision.

And of course, thank you, everyone who reads "Homefront" in the Plainfield Sun newspaper. You certainly don't have to. That you continue to do so is both surprising and flattering.

Contents

Chocolate Cows and Purple Cheese

What will they write about me?

The Illinois Fatherhood Initiative, the country's only statewide nonprofit organization aimed at helping men be better fathers and father figures annually sponsors a statewide Father's Day essay contest on the theme, "What My Father Means to Me."

As I helped read through thousands of essays recently, I found myself wondering -- and worrying -- what my two daughters might one day write about me and my fathering.

Will they have a sense of the intense demands of fatherhood, indeed parenthood today? Or, as in a disturbing number of the essays, will they be happy merely because I go to work and -- epitomizing the shallow 1990s -- occasionally buy them stuff?

Will they describe the man who makes them laugh with silly answers (both truth and tall-tales) to their questions? Actual examples:

Q. "Dad, how do you make chocolate ice cream?"

A. "You find a chocolate cow, put it in the freezer and then squish the ice cream out." (Tall-tale)

Q. "Dad, what did I look like when I was born?"

A. "A big ball of purple cheese." (True)

Or will they write about the man who quashes their fun much too often by saying "No," "Not now," and "Later"?

Will I be portrayed as the dad who loves to read to them before bed, and has stocked their library for years to come? Or the one who gets grumpy when their bedrooms are a mess?

In their minds, am I the dad who taught them to play baseball and "wrassle," or the kind who can't seem to find enough time to play with them as much as they'd like?

Am I the dad who helps them say their nighttime prayers and lets them take turns saying grace at dinner? Or the one who sometimes slips and uses certain colorful swear phrases?

When they write about me, will I be the dad who pines all day long at work to hear their sweet, boisterous, silly laughter burst from their smiling faces? Or the one who needs – begs for -- a few minutes of peace once I get home to gear back up to their explosive, high-energy pace?

Will they portray me as the dad who can't wait to hold, hug, kiss and tickle them? Or the one who reluctantly spanks them when all other discipline fails to gain their attention?

Unfortunately for them (but fortunately for the mental health industry, I'm sure) I am all of these fathers, and more.

I am a modern dad.

I encourage my kids to ignore all bounds, and guide their efforts to succeed, however they define success. I publicly praise, support and love my wife so that our kids know we are parenting partners. There will be no pitting Mom against Dad.

And, as girls heading into the new millennium, I especially want them to know that "cave" doesn't always precede "man:" I'm not ashamed to cry in front of them or apologize for my shortcomings.

I openly share my faith in a God who loves us. I wasn't uncomfortable in the delivery room. I had no problem changing diapers. And I am happy to help clean the house and do the laundry.

Yet, my patience is a short fuse igniting an often-flaming temper. I adore my children. But sometimes I'd give my left arm to buy my wife and me a quick spin in the Time Machine to our PK (Pre-Kids) days.

Too often, my behavior is fueled by my foolish, "Tom-centric" belief that the world would be a better place if everyone would do things my way. And I am too quick to hold my family accountable for slights committed by others.

In the end, I suppose, I can do only what I can: try to do my best, and fix what needs fixing so that I can be the best dad possible. For them. For my wife. For myself. When my kids write about me, hopefully they'll see -- and say -- that I did at least this much.

Meanwhile, I have to work on another explanation for chocolate ice cream. The girls are a little dubious about my frozen cow theory.

Still Dreaming

President Barack Obama has accomplished many things in his relatively young life.

But one thing that he hasn't done, is end racism.

Nor can he -- though it seems some people think he has done so. Some seem to believe – or wish? -- that just because an African American has been elected president, that racism is no longer a problem in our great country.

That the headaches and heartaches caused by racial and ethnic-based hatred, confusion and fear have somehow magically become non-issues.

Sadly, nothing could be further from the truth.

About 53 percent of voters who cast a ballot last November voted for Obama. Wouldn't it be great to say that all of those people voted for Obama because they were racially enlightened?

But the polls told us that a lot of that majority voted for Obama because they were sick enough of the Republican party, turned off enough by John McCain, insulted enough by Sarah Palin, or angry enough about any number of other matters to ignore their own racism and vote for a black man.

We ended up at the right place. But that doesn't mean we got there the right way, nor that we have no need for further intellectual, philosophical and spiritual travel together.

In fact, if we as an American society were at all wise, at all honest, at all brave, we would use Obama's most significant accomplishment to date as a platform to dive headlong into the deep end of the issue of racism, once and for all.

We would confront our misperceptions, our lingering suspicions of "those people" (whoever they may be for each of us), and have the kind of courageous conversations that need to occur to better understand, appreciate and even celebrate each other's differences.

Only by admitting and accepting what separates us – and you have to love the irony of this -- will we be able to finally, truly, sincerely come together.

A recent Newsweek magazine article titled "Rethinking Race In the Classroom" raised the point that some people in and around education want to stop teaching "Huck Finn" and end Black History Month, all because Barack Obama is now president.

The article quotes Todd Boyd, who teaches race and popular culture at the University of Southern California: "I think there is a certain sector of the country that now feels racism is over, let's move on," Boyd said.

Indeed, it seems that some people who think this way – including many who voted for the new president – are using his election as a way to assuage their own guilt

– it is not unreasonable to call it "white guilt" since 43 percent of white voters supported Obama.

I can almost hear them saying, "Ok, that's that. We voted for a black person. Cross racism off the list…"

But it's not that easy.

We cannot as a country now pretend that 400 years of racially-based hatred, societal fear mongering, and systemic injustice didn't happen; that the sting of racism is no longer felt, and therefore racism should no longer be a top priority concern, just because of one glorious day.

President Obama himself during his campaign called for more open dialogue about racism and the role race has played in our country's history.

That is, admittedly, one mean, tough, scary neighborhood to visit.

Still, we must do so no matter how frightening, embarrassing, or discomforting. Honest, open dialogue is the only way to get behind the curtain of fear and learn that there's really nothing to be afraid of.

In another part of my life, I work with a dear friend and mentor who talks about the need to seek and accept "comfort with discomfort" about our inherent national and personal racism.

She says that we must be willing, from both sides of the issue, to acknowledge and address the very large elephant in the room. In America, that elephant continues to be racism.

It's nice to dream of a world in which people of all races, ethnicities, sexual orientations, physical conditions, religious beliefs, etc. all get along.

But reality then slaps us, hard, across our pink and

brown and black faces, and we wake up to the world as it really is.

In that world – in our world – we must continue to look at ourselves in the mirror, to confront each and every ugly pimple, so that we might one day be as beautiful as we are in our dreams.

In this case, that means continuing to admit, study, and work against our country's racist history. We must confront our past so that can figure out how to change our present and future. How does the saying go? If we ignore our history, we are doomed to repeat it?

Yes, we are better than what we were. Having elected Barack Obama to the presidency proves that beyond measure.

But we are not yet what we want to be.

<u>Proving God with Helping Hands</u>

"To Kellie, Emma, and Olivia: You prove God."

That's the dedication that tops my tiny collection of poetry. Maybe it will be published someday, if only on a blog somewhere in cyberspace.

The dedication's meaning is simple, if not immediately clear.

I am not saying that my marriage or the birth of our children was in any way divine.

As it is for many, marriage for me was the result of a happy accident. I blindly stumbled into a relationship with a wonderful woman and have been (marginally) smart enough to not screw it up too badly (yet.)

Likewise, my kids are truly the most precious gifts in my world. Their births were and remain far and away the most awesome moments in my life. But they were examples of routine biology and modern medical professionalism, not miracles.

Still, all three of them prove God's existence to me every day, because they embody what I understand and believe God to be: not some ethereal being "out there", but rather the essence of love, charity, empathy, and the exuberance of life, inside of us all.

With Christmas only a few days away my sincere and solemn prayer is that we each find someone who proves God for us and more, that we each prove God to someone else.

Along with exasperating conservatives, my favorite hobby is studying what I call historical theology.

I am fascinated by the human melodrama encompassed in the evolution of faith in a higher being; the development of the numerous religious systems that encapsulate that faith; and the mutation of said systems into assorted denominations and subgroups.

What a strange journey it has been...

My favorite author in this avocation is retired Episcopalian Bishop John Shelby Spong.

In his many books, Spong makes one point consistently: that the kingdom of God is not located in some heaven above the clouds. Rather, the kingdom that Jesus lived and espoused, is in and among all of us.

We humans carry the kingdom of heaven in our hearts and souls.

We make heaven real through our relationships with each other.

That was the stunningly simple, yet life-altering complex message of Jesus' life – a message so radical that it has still to settle and take hold even 2,000 years later.

In a chapter in his most recent book, "A New Christianity for a New World," Spong writes, "Incarnation is not just a fact about Jesus. It is a symbol of how God, who is the source of life, love, and being, operates. God was in Christ, reconciling. God is in me. God is in you, reconciling, healing, restoring, making whole."

If it is to thrive, our community, like all communities, must make itself whole by learning the value and necessity of placing others over self.

We must commit ourselves as a community to doing the work of community: caring for others, giving selflessly, leading with the greater good in mind despite gratification delayed and delayed and delayed.

And why? Selflessly, selfishly, ironically, because our own survival may depend on it.

Don't fret. The tools for this timely and timeless endeavor are already in place.

Our governmental leaders are dedicated to systemically serving and protecting our communal interests. Help them by participating in and supporting the system.

Charitable organizations aim to aid and comfort the less fortunate. Help them by generously donating your time, talents and treasures. Remember that people are just as hungry and poor and needy after the holidays as during.

Churches stand by to guide people in their search for higher meaning, ethical and moral clarity, and spiritual connection. Help them by leading by example. Be a regular shadow in their doorways, and bring a few others with you.

The value of strong community is intrinsic and indisputable. But finding and defining that value is not easy. It requires work. It demands commitment.

It depends on ones willingness to live fully the life given to us by God – however you understand and call God – by loving, caring for, and nurturing those around you, including, especially, those who do not look or think or talk or act like you.

As Spong wrote, "It is our shared being that binds us powerfully into a human community."

This Christmas and beyond, for the sake of ourselves and each other, for this community and community everywhere, let's all try to "prove God."

Truth, with a Capital "T"

I'm a mess.

My brain and spirit have been in a head-on collision over the recent Northern Illinois University shooting. Between the real-life chaos and heartbreak caused by the gunman, and the metaphoric twisted wreckage of my ideals and thoughts, lies my convoluted soul.

I am a card-carrying member of the ACLU. Literally. My member card is tucked into my wallet right behind the reminder of my next dental appointment.

To the core of my being I believe that every person, regardless of their race, color, creed, socioeconomic status, gender, sexual orientation, political affiliation, age, hair cut, fashion sense or eye color, has the same inalienable rights laid out in our Constitution.

You remember the Constitution? The one document that guarantees our basic freedoms and protections, at least in theory, if not always in practice. Among those rights is the presumption of innocence, and the right to a fair trial.

These insurances are Truths, with a capital "T". Unchanging. Absolute. Non-negotiable.

Not subject to interpretation or selective application by anyone. And that includes whoever is sitting behind the desk in the Oval Office.

Without this bedrock belief, America is no better than any third-rate, street-punk dictatorship that pretends to be free – right up until the time such supposed freedom becomes inconvenient for the dictator du jour.

What makes America great is not that we protect the strong, rich, honest and powerful. That's easy. But that we protect the weak, poor, dishonest and powerless.

Soft-hearted? Naïve? Silly? Perhaps.

But that's the real beauty of our system. That the lowest, meanest, cheatingest, snivelingest, nastiest crook is afforded the same rights as your dear, loving mother.

And yet, and yet, and yet…

After former NIU graduate student Steven Kazmierczak gunned down five innocent people and injured 16 more on February 14, 2008 – a new Valentines Day massacre -- the first thoughts through my head were not to ensure his civil liberties.

In my heart, I continued to insist that he is (or was, since he killed himself – the supreme act of cowardice) an American and deserves the same protections as anyone else, including the assumption of innocence and the right to a fair trial.

But my brain was taking a U-turn, careening toward a mental off-ramp that has been under construction since the Columbine massacre in 1999.

In my mind, I no longer cared about Kazmierczak's

civil rights. My thoughts ran more to the broader idea of human rights.

I care about your human rights – I care about you as a human being – precisely until you stop acting like a human being. In this case, exactly until Kazmierczak pulled the trigger.

Up to that moment, I cared that he was, apparently, a victim of mental illness, in a broad, we-are-all-connected-through-God kind of way.

That perhaps he was depressed. That maybe his life had somehow, in some way only he could explain, spun wildly into darkness. That demons had invaded his own spirit, telling him that his own life wasn't worth living.

And I remain willing, as a member of a caring Christian community to extend a hand of grace to such souls. To help foot the societal bill for their care and eventual recovery and wellness.

Until the first bullet flew.

At that point he forfeited his human rights by forfeiting his humanity -- by inflicting his own pain on others who had not caused, and therefore did not deserve, his anguish.

It breaks my heart to confess these thoughts. I am ashamed. Concerned. Frightened. Not because I elevate myself to some pedestal, but because I have always believed, assumed – hoped? -- that others felt the way I do.

Does this vigilante-esque, self-centered change of heart somehow make me less caring? Less Christian? Less American?

Less human?

And if my own feelings can change so radically, what does that mean for others, and for the world around us?

I recognize people's imperfections. But I don't understand the need to hurt. That includes the death penalty. The human state doesn't grant life. Therefore it doesn't have the right to take it.

But then I look at my wife and daughters. The three people who make my own otherwise-goofy life worth living.

And I know that as much as I believe in civil rights for all, I believe in civil rights for them, first and foremost. And no one will rob them of their rights without a fight from me.

That is also a Truth, with a capital "T". Unchanging, absolute, non-negotiable.

Sweetie and the Jerk

Giving new, and sad, meaning to the phrase, "the dog days of summer"…

I am a man of many faults.

Short on patience, long on temper, quick to criticize and slow to trust. Demanding, expecting excellence from everyone, including myself. Sarcastic and judgmental, cynical. That's me, in a slightly-paranoid nutshell

Basically, I can be a living, breathing jerk.

Still, three key facts save me from my many shortcomings:

1. I sincerely believe in a higher power in our lives – call it God;
2. I believe that God embodies true love, redeems us with that love and expects and empowers us to share it with all living things;
3. I see such ideals modeled daily by people who are much more authentically "Christian" than me, most especially my wife and children.

Still, even at my jerk-jerk-jerkiest, I wouldn't abandon my family pet.

Early one recent Saturday morning, my wife took our eldest daughter to her summer job. Passing a park along the way, they noticed a small dog, a Yorkshire terrier mix, running loose in the parking lot near a garbage can.

Being the kind soul she is, my wife stopped. No one was in sight. The dog, all 10 pounds of it – including the extra pound of dirt embedded in its matted, stinking fur -- was scared and confused.

Afraid the dog might get hit trying to cross the street, she finally coaxed it into the car (my car, by the way) where it promptly pooped on the passenger seat (my passenger seat, by the way.)

She came home, woke me, told me what had happened, and asked what we should do. "We?" I thought. "What do you mean, 'We'? 'We' didn't pick up a stray dog. And 'We' wasn't just awoken from a very sound sleep following a long overnight shift at his part-time job."

Luckily, in a rare display of judicious self-editing, I didn't say any of that.

What I did say, though, wasn't very helpful either.

My first concern, typically, was not for this little dog, but for the inconvenience it would cause on an already-overstuffed weekend.

Our two nieces had spent the night. One daughter was working her summer job that morning. The other was scheduled to baby-sit from 5 p.m. to midnight. I had my usual list of weekend yard work, errands and chores.

We had plans for lunch with all four kids at the Ace drive-in restaurant in Joliet. And I had to work another eight-hour graveyard shift that night.

Not to mention that our own dog is scared of most other pooches and now was effectively trapped in the house, since my wife had tied up the uninvited visitor in the back yard. And now, we had to deal with a stray dog?

See? I fly quickly to jerk-hood.

Instead, I should have been thinking about the well-being of this dog – as indeed were my wife, youngest daughter and both nieces.

"Sweetie," as my wife took to calling the dog, had a collar, but no tags. It was well fed and appeared fairly healthy, if very dirty. And, after spraying it off a bit, it was obvious the dog had been groomed. Sadly, it seemed clear as day that the little thing had been left in the park.

I suggested taking it back to the park in case someone was looking for it there. Admittedly, the suggestion was made as much for my sake – to get rid of the thing – as for the dog's.

However, my wife, St. Kellie, the Thoughtful, Patient, Wise and Ever Compassionate, had better ideas.

She reached out for help to our dear and best friends who are both veterinarians, as well as our own dog's groomer. She called several area police departments and animal control facilities and shelters. Finally, mid-afternoon, we found one in Shorewood willing to take Sweetie.

Importantly, it was a "no-kill" facility. No one – most especially our youngest niece, whose picture is in the dictionary under the definition of "animal lover" -- wanted anything to happen to this dog after the ordeal it had suffered.

We delivered the dog to the shelter.

Nearly two weeks later, we can only assume and hope that Sweetie was adopted by a caring family. Perhaps one whose parents have taught their little kids the true meaning of kindness.

No one and nothing should ever have to endure the hardship this poor dog did. Except for the person who left her out at that park.

That person was a true jerk.

Sure, Honey, I'll Get to That, In Just a Few Minutes...

Ok, this is it.

Writing this piece is probably the last thing I can do this weekend to avoid installing the new garbage disposal. But I'll have to really stretch it out. Pretend like it's a real think piece to take it right up to dinner time. Then, after dinner, I'll have to make sure I do an extra-good job of cleaning up, including vacuuming.

I've run the gamut of stall tactics and delays to avoid this particular chore. Work brought home from the office successfully pushed my Saturday morning chores to Saturday afternoon. Then I invited my wife to watch a long cowboy movie Saturday night.

When she went to bed early into the movie (she was being very sweet and indulgent to actually even sit down with me, cowboys not being her favorite thing) I tacked on two episodes of "NYPD Blue" Season Three from my DVD collection.

Well, I certainly couldn't install the thing at 1 a.m.

now, could I? That would have been terribly inconsiderate on my part, and I do love my family.

Sunday, I slept a little later than normal. After all, I'd been up until the wee hours watching television…Then I did more of my work from the office until the early afternoon.

Then I snuggled up with our youngest daughter to watch "Jurassic Park." She's a burgeoning film buff, So I felt it was my duty as a parent – her first and best teacher -- to share this Spielberg classic with her. Especially since the lessons she learns from me now could help make her very wealthy down the road -- if she ever takes up filmmaking, that is.

I stopped the movie several times to explain this film technique and that directorial choice.

"You see how he didn't show the dinosaurs immediately?" I prompted my daughter. "He did that to create suspense. What you have to imagine for yourself is always scarier than what you can see. Spielberg learned that from Alfred Hitchcock," I tutored.

"Like the shark in 'Jaws'?" she said. Exactly! See? Sitting on the couch for another two hours was paying off big. It wasn't just to avoid doing a job for which I am ill-equipped. My daughter could end up being the Next Great Movie Director because of my dedication and guidance…

Well, after all that educating, I was tired again. So a nice Sunday afternoon nap with my wife followed.

And so, here we are. As I type, she's in the kitchen making dinner. If I play my cards just right, that garbage disposal will have to wait until next weekend, which is just fine with me.

I blame my dad for this short-coming.

Before you go accusing me of some kind of Freudian flimflam, let me explain that my dad wasn't very good at what some might call, in a sexist way, "manly chores."

He was a great cop, and a very good father, and a decent husband. But ask him to paint a room, change the oil, fix the brakes on a car, build anything requiring more than a few nails or some glue?

Let's just say that if he were still alive today, he might star in a reality show called "Tony's Fix-It Shop – You Want it Done Right, This Isn't the Place."

Subsequently, I've spent my adult life asking others to help me. I've relied on the kindness of friends (unpaid) and strangers (paid) to complete projects like installing a chair railing, putting in attic stairs, making minor car repairs, laying the hardwood floors in our house, and numerous other tasks that men are supposedly genetically encoded to be able to do.

The good news is, I've learned to do a thing or two. I can swing a decent hammer and use a circular saw without embarrassing myself too badly. And my wife says I look pretty hot in my tool belt. That's something…

Better yet, I've built some strong friendships with the guys who have tolerated my lack of handy-manliness, and taught me a thing or two. So I guess I do have some "construction" skills – though they're more social than industrial.

Truth be told, the garbage disposal installation is pretty straight-forward. At least it looks that way on paper.

Problem is, I have to turn off the power to the house

to disconnect the old disposal and hook up the new one. And electricity makes me very nervous.

Hey, look at that! My wife is calling us to dinner, and the clock on the wall is chiming "too late to put in a garbage disposal today." Success! Well, there's always next Saturday. As long as my buddy Alex can help.

But I have to give blood next Saturday. And take my girls to their grandparents, get the car washed, write a script for a play I'm in…

My Kingdom for an Old Tree

That's it. I want an old tree.

An old tree. A tree with more rings than Ringo Starr. A tree with some wisdom. A tree with some stature.

Fall is by far my favorite season, and that's partly because of the changing leaves. This year's event has been particularly spectacular because of all the rain in September.

So one recent day as I was driving into town I was really taken by the breathtaking beauty of some of the trees lining the streets coming into the village.

That's when the tree envy really hit.

You see, we who live in the numerous newer subdivisions filling out this area generally do not have such amenities.

We have new houses. We have new neighbors. New schools. New parks. New, new, new.

And for the most part we have big sticks masquerading as trees, fertilized by developers' promises that one day, those sticks will gently cover our yards with brilliant gold and red and brown blankets as they prepare for their winter's nap.

Now, generally speaking, new is good.

New means better insulation and lower heating bills. New means warranties. New means younger teachers sparked by fresh ideas and methods.

But when it comes to trees, new means nothing.

There certainly won't be much jumping into piles of leaves recently fallen from new trees. What leaves?

When my wife and I bought our (new) house my mom got us a leaf blower.

At first I thought it was a joke. A leaf blower? We didn't need a machine to clean up our leaves. We didn't have leaves. We had leaf. The job could be done with a single rake in less than a quarter of a Bears game.

Some developers recognize the intrinsic spiritual, communal and financial value of an amenity like an old tree. Respecting the spiritual and communal, particularly as it relates to the financial, they'll build their houses around such trees, and jack up the prices of their product accordingly.

And there's definitely something to be said for what an old tree can do for ones property value.

Trees that have survived decades, even scores of years, of lightning, fire, bugs – and developers – testify to the power of nature to preserver. "You can do what you want, build what you want, but I'm not going anywhere," they seem to say.

They remind us in a time when everything changes before we can even get used to it, that there's real meaning, true weight, unique value, to age and experience. And they say that some things just don't change.

But many developers tear down such trees to build as many houses as possible and then – the ultimate paradox -- replace them later with saplings.

Now, there's nothing wrong with a young tree. It speaks of the promise of the future. A time when children and grandchildren will define our lives, rather than mortgage payments and minivans.

But it's awfully hard to sit in the branches of a sapling.

It's nearly impossible to build a tree house in something that's only as tall as you are.

And it's really dangerous to try to swing from branches that can barely support the weight of their springtime buds.

I like where I live. And I don't want to move.

I like that we're building a new life with people like us, living lives like ours.

We watch over and care for each other's children. We wave to each other in the school halls. We laugh about our battles with tomato plants and compare honey-do lists.

I understand new.

But I really, really look forward to the day when we can grouse and commiserate about our hassles and joys under an old tree.

<u>Chapter One: Shut Up and Listen To Your Wife</u>

Finally, 3,649 days later, I've figured it out.

For nearly 10 years of married life, I've been trying to convince my wife that it's not just me. When I tell her, for example that she has to turn off the light on her side of the bed, I'm not being lazy or just pulling something out of some arbitrary hat of rules.

I'm quoting the "Young Marrieds Handbook."

The handbook is a very useful tool for fairly arbitrating any marital dispute. It's intended mainly for couples still learning how to walk the tightrope of marriage as they adjust to their partners' many quirks.

But the handbook's guidelines are just as useful down the road when the adventure of discovery congeals into gelatinous complacency.

For some reason though, the handbook never seemed to have the desired effect. In debate after dispute I'd cite it to bolster my point. But my wife rarely saw its inherent logic. Probably because I had not yet committed it to print.

Well, tomorrow is our 10th wedding anniversary and Saturday we are renewing our wedding vows. So now's as good a time as any to jot down some of the handbook's key points:

***Never make fun of your partner's choice in (pick one) music, television, books or movies. Even if he/she thinks the Brady kids were a hoot and doesn't recognize the superior comic brilliance of Arnold the Pig from "Green Acres."

***Remember, toothpaste tubes have bottoms for a reason – to be squeezed. Don't touch the middle until it becomes the bottom. Likewise, there is indeed a difference between "over" and "under" when it comes to toilet paper. Learn your partner's preference and honor it.

***Always side with your spouse in all contests of skill – especially family and social disputes. Remember, you chose each other. You didn't choose your parents, siblings or in-laws.

***Never question why your partner continues to support (insert your favorite sports team here) despite their ongoing futility. Statements like "I don't know why you bother to keep watching" as the Bears/Bulls/Cubs/Sox/Blackhawks gets stomped yet again do little to engender love and affection.

***Remember, it's only money. It really doesn't matter how much he/she manages to squeeze in between phone calls to family and friends that he/she could have (and probably did) talk to earlier that day. It's the cathartic quality of the experience for your partner. A good telephone call makes for a happy partner, and a happy partner makes for a happy you. Of course, a good telephone call pack also saves a lot of heartache.

***So what if your partner likes Spam, grits and okra? Believe it or not, lots of people do. That doesn't necessarily make me – er, I mean, him or her -- weird.

*** No, your partner can't resist the urge to flip through all 99 channels during every commercial break. Yes, he/she does need to watch for the thousandth time the episode of "Little House on the Prairie" in which Laura falls for her future husband, "Manly." So what if he/she can recite entire hunks of "Ben Hur." Get over it.

***When choosing children's names, remember how viciously creative little kids can be with initials, nicknames and such. Aunt Mildred and Uncle Mortimer will get over the hurt of their names not being carried on through another generation, and your children will love you forever.

***It won't kill you to help with the laundry/dinner/cleaning/yard work.

***If you promise to be home by 6 p.m., be home by 5:45 p.m., not 6:30 p.m. The job will be there tomorrow. If you're always late, your spouse may not be.

***Watching your own kids so that your spouse can take a well-deserved break does not constitute "babysitting." You helped make them, you can help watch them.

***Above all, remember that laughter and love go hand in hand -- as you always should when walking in public.

There it is, the first chapter of the "Young Marrieds Handbook." Now on to Chapter Two: "The Battle of the Bulge…"

Calling Mr. Fix-it…

What really surprised me wasn't that my father-in-law tried to get a television repaired, but rather the idea that there are television repairmen left to call.

Then, as if God wanted to confirm this seeming incongruity, I found myself this past weekend lugging my six-month-old vacuum cleaner to a repairman.

It's not that the machine itself is so wonderful that it deserves saving. I am thoroughly disappointed by it.

To someone who finds vacuuming therapeutic, as I do, a bad vacuum cleaner is like a bad relationship – it makes you suspicious of every other person – er, I mean, vacuum cleaner – who comes along.

To put it plainly, if we hadn't paid several hundred dollars for it only this past spring, and Christmas weren't quickly and methodically nibbling away at our budget, this thing would have been sucking its way to vacuum heaven – or hell as the case may be – as fast as I could roll it out to the curb.

The sad reality is, we live in a disposable world.

Anything that can be and is made, can be and is made to be thrown away. Hence, my surprise at learning there are television and vacuum cleaner repairmen still at work.

That may strike some as the height of convenience in the fast-paced days. Value is important, sure, but cost tops all concerns. Cheap, fast and easy often – usually -- wins out over more costly, slow and challenging.

Which is precisely the problem.

Why bother repairing anything when it is so much easier (and often less expensive) to simply go buy another one? When something wears out or breaks, or even, heaven forbid, grows tiresome, too difficult or no longer draws our eye as it once did, we simply throw it away.

This is true with every kind of material good – furniture, clothing, appliances, electronics. I myself am guilty of buying three replacement DVD players to replace the original when it broke, only to see them break too.

The cause was as obvious as the price tag. It was easier to simply buy a new DVD player because they were so cheap. And they were cheap, because they were cheaply made. And "cheaply made" breaks easily. But I could replace it every time it broke because it was cheap…a vicious circle if ever there was one.

Worse yet than this dizzying, spiraling materialism, is that many of us treat our relationships the same way.

This is no wonder, really.

The same mindset that would rather throw away a vacuum or television than do the work and sacrifice and pay the cost of investing in a good one to start with, is the same mindset that will run from a challenge or ignore a problem rather than address it honestly, thoughtfully and caringly.

We have come to treat the people around us like the material goods which we consume, and which consume us.

We'd rather get divorced than do the hard work necessary to repair and maintain a solid relationship.

We'd rather throw away people who disagree with us, than respect their position.

We'd rather kick to the curb people who look or speak differently, rather than appreciate their diversity.

We'd rather avert our eyes from the poor, the hungry, the lost, the hurt, the angry in our world, because helping them is inconvenient.

Finding, creating and maintaining quality in anything, be it a product or a relationship, takes time. Energy. Perseverance. Sympathy. Empathy. None of these is easy. But none of them are impossible, either.

We should be more frugal and thoughtful about what we buy.

We should make quality, not convenience, our top priority.

We should invest in things that will last. And do what is necessary to make sure that they endure. Appreciate the craftsmanship, the hard work, the commitment that went into their making.

Things break. That's to be expected. What's more important though is that when they do, we be dedicated enough to fix them. This might cost more in the short run, but it'll save us in the long run.

In this way, we can all be repairmen. And our relationships, homes and community – if not necessarily our vacuums and televisions -- will be the better for it.

Yoopers, Yah Hey…

We are Yoopers, proud and true. We are Yoopers, through and through.

And if you don't know what a Yooper is, well, you've never experienced the thrill of a 200-pound black bear traipsing inches away from your pillow at 1 a.m.

We have, while camping in the Great North Woods that is Michigan's Upper Peninsula, or UP.

Lowlanders – which are basically anyone not from the UP – are called, not always fondly, Yoopers. The locals may mean it somewhat derisively. But we love the place so much that we're glad to wear the tag as a badge of honor.

Frankly, we've been going to the UP so long that it might be fair to even consider us honorary homers, eh? And we're going again.

First, we tool through central Wisconsin, about half way to Copper Harbor, Michigan, the northern-most point in the state – the edge of the nail of the "finger" of land that extends into Lake Superior.

A half mile further up the road, you either turn around and point your vehicle toward Miami, 1,400 miles in the other direction, or prepare to take a chilly dip in the 55-degree water.

My wife has been making this trip most of her life. I joined the caravan when I joined her family. I've not regretted doing either, not even once.

Growing up on the east side of Joliet, the son of a sheriff's deputy who had never known the Great Outdoors himself, the closest I'd ever been to camping was sleeping in a makeshift tent at my maternal grandparents' house. They lived on a farm in Herscher, Illinois, a fly speck near Kankakee.

We spent practically every weekend there until they moved to Arkansas when I was 15. So I knew something about living in the country.

I was a little bit country and a little bit rock-and-roll (not to mention jazz and rhythm and blues) years before Donnie and Marie Osmond hit on the idea.

I loved waking up to the dulcet tones – and not-so-dulcet smells -- of the cows and chickens at the farm across the road. Riding with my Uncle Gene on his Suzuki motorcycle up and down the country road, no house nor human for a mile in either direction.

Playing in the barn. Having dirt clod fights in the fields with my Uncles Mike and Brian, who were close enough in age to be more big brothers than uncles. Slopping and feeding the pigs my grandfather bought and named after us.

But the country is not the same as the Great Outdoors.

Camping was an entirely foreign experience that first

time. Not so much for sleeping outside, which I'd done before on the farm.

Rather, because of the absence of night noises. Growing up, trains rattled a block away, or a farmhouse full of people raised a ruckus most of the night. Not being able to see anything – literally, nothing – in front of my face at night was also new. Streetlights and nightlights had illuminated my childhood.

And the void of organized time.

On the farm, there was always, always, always something to do. When camping though, you either learn to fill your own time, or do nothing.

And, oh by the way, the sun doesn't go down until 10 p.m. So there is no deadline. No urgency. No rush to do anything at all. There is, always, no time and plenty of time at the same time.

Honestly, it was unnerving.

To a young man used to being busy every minute – swaddled in a thin blanket of Catholic guilt about any kind of "idle" time – having nothing to do (or worse, doing nothing on purpose) just didn't sit well with my conscience.

It was especially discombobulating when our kids were younger. I constantly felt the pressure of being "Dad". Of having to entertain them and account for their time, too.

For several years, I'd need the first few days of vacation to unwind so that I could enjoy my vacation. Now though, after setting up camp, I take off my watch and settle easily into a routine of non-routine.

People ask what we do when we are away, and I proudly say, "nothing."

We play games. We ride bikes. We eat some of the best ice cream ever made. We hike. We dip our toes in the lake.

Or we hunt agates along the beach. Or visit the restored Civil War fort. Or ride to the top of Brockway Mountain and take in one of the most breathtaking views anywhere – a reminder that God really knows how to wield a paint brush.

The key is, whatever we do, including doing nothing, we do together.

I don't know if being a Yooper makes us better people. But certainly it lets us breathe better air. Rest a little more. Stress a little less. And that can't be bad.

Six O'Quock, Always Six O'Quock

I have never been more aware of the tick-tock ticking of the clock than I have in the last few weeks.

For some reason known only to God and other 3-year-olds, my youngest daughter, Olivia has been fascinated by time lately.

Throughout the day she will ask, "Daddy, what time it is?" I will tell her. Then, as if my wife wanted or needed to know, she'll turn to Kellie and announce, dutifully, "Mom, it's (whatever time I told her.)"

But, if anyone asks her the time, she invariably answers, in her slightly-slurred, lisping, twisted post-toddler syntax, "Is six o'quock." Which, I've realized, means I'm either very late, or very early.

It's easy to laugh at my daughter's slightly exasperating awareness of the clock. But as I've tried to solve the mystery of her fixation on all things temporal, it occurred to me that time is a big part of all parents' lives with their children.

A recent e-mail from a friend reminded me of how

little time we really have, and how much we waste on concerns we flatter ourselves into believing are critical, but which really are frivolous.

We spend too much time making money instead of making friends; buying stuff instead of building relationships; talking, instead of listening.

We push people away instead of pulling them near. We constantly look ahead instead of looking around. We seek the smell of success rather than the scent of roses.

We commit ourselves to so much outside activity that we have nothing left for what's inside of us. We meet to plan meetings to plan planning meetings. As the e-mail said, "we've added years to life, but not life to years."

Time wasted is time lost.

So the next time Olivia asks me what time it is, I will tell myself: It's time to work a little less and play a little more.

It's time to eat a good meal together at home, holding hands as we pray. It's time to read one more story before tucking her and Winnie the Pooh into bed.

It's time to forgo another episode of (insert your favorite television show here) and break out Chutes and Ladders, Don't Break the Ice, Candy Land or, if you're really ambitious and limber, Twister.

It's time to listen to her explain yet again, no matter how hard I must try to keep a straight face, how her doll spent the day battling the "flute."

It's time to share the proper tooth brushing techniques so that her million-dollar smile will always be as bright as it is now. It's time to shave our "wikkers" together; though she usually manages to get more shaving cream on the vanity than on her face.

It's time to patiently hold her tightly in my arms when the storm-driven wind plays the drainpipe like a clarinet. I know that it's just another spring squall, but in her young, active imagination, every window-rattling breeze is an Oz-ian tornado.

It's time to take a day off of work in the middle of the week to visit the zoo, or museum, or simply to ride bikes to the park.

But most of all, it's time to tell her, as often as I can, that I love, respect and cherish her more than any man ever will.

For I know that, soon enough, she'll be too big for me to flip onto my shoulder. She won't want to hold my hand in public. She will pretend she didn't hear me ask for a kiss goodbye as she spills out of the car on her way to rendezvous with her friends.

Too soon, young men will be fascinated by the paradoxical combination of her delicate beauty and her vexing, "I-double-dog-dare-you-to-tell-me-no" personality. Many of those boys will run away, I am sure. But eventually, one won't.

Then, she'll have less time for me.

I will be sad, certainly. But I am assured, if not entirely comforted by the knowledge that the process is all a part of who we are supposed to be.

And I know that if I properly manage time now, the clock will later bring memories, and smiles.

I'll B Ur BFF If U'l Stp Txtng

Finally!

After years of strenuous research, painstaking observation, careful contemplation and exhaustive (and exhausting) mental noodling, I stumbled upon a numerical expression of the difference between my generation and today's teenagers.

Here it is:

9,004.

That is the number of text messages sent and/or received last month by my eldest daughter, the fruit of my loins, whom I love dearly. (I keep saying things like this to remind myself that she is, basically redeemable and good, and that kid-o-cide is frowned upon…)

Meanwhile, my wife, another fine representative of the 40-something crowd, sent and/or received 19 text messages.

Nineteen. And most of those were probably in response to our daughter!

Thinking maybe this was the final, undeniable

confirmation that I need bifocals, I removed my glasses just to be sure I was seeing what I thought I was seeing. Sadly, my eyes were not deceiving me.

Nine thousand and four.

That's about five text messages sent or received every minute, if math serves. Or five mini-conversations and/or responses crammed into every minute, every day for 30 days.

Yet, when I mentioned this to my wife and daughters, none of them was fazed. After all, they told me, text messaging is how kids communicate today.

Gone, I suppose, are the "good old days" of passing hand-written notes to friends. Of waiting your turn for the phone and then stretching the telephone cord into your bedroom to chat for hours. (I can just hear my kids now: "Telephone cord? What's that?")

Now, anyone old enough to move their thumbs up and down has their own cell phone. They use these calamitous communicators to talk, text, surf the Web, get directions, watch movies and order dinner, even beam up to spaceships if they have the right service pack.

My daughters and most of their peers have grown up in a Cell Phone World. They know nothing else.

Once, in a nostalgic mood shaded by frustration over the ubiquity of cell phones, my wife and I told the girls that telephones used to be connected to the wall. And that the handsets were connected to the base by a wire.

There was no walking from room to room unless you had a 100-foot cord. There was no losing the phone under the couch cushion, paging each other from room to room, etc.

And shock of shocks, there was actually a time before

"call waiting." If your BFF (that's "best friend forever" for you really old fogies) called and your dad was on the phone, that other caller – gasp! – heard a busy signal and – double gasp! – actually had to call back!

By the horrified looks on their faces you would have thought our heads had fallen off and spilled into the spaghetti.

I don't want to sound like a complete curmudgeon. Nor do I mean to suggest, like so many older folks, that the "good old days" were always better. Far from it.

For example, though I remember it, I cannot imagine a world without personal computers. Technology has and does and will make our lives easier, more exciting and even more efficient (when it works, that is.)

Yes, I am older. But I am not old.

Yet I am also not a techno-geek.

I don't wet my pants every time Apple guru Steve Jobs burps twice. I find the commercials with the Mac Guy and the Windows Guy mildly amusing, but you won't find me sparring with anyone over which operating system is better.

Frankly, I think people who charge out to buy The Next Big Thing are foolish and pretentious.

I'm usually a little behind the techno curve. But I'm also not wasting money on the latest silicone-chipped fad. Give it a year or two. The price will drop like a rock.

So here I am, squarely in the middle of middle age.

Amazed, awed and somewhat irritated by the younger generation's insistence on moving life forward whether I (we) like it or not.

Concerned that my kids' thumbs will crumble at the

joint and fall off from texting so much, ruining the fit of every pair of gloves they have.

Frustrated by how distant this new technology makes us as human beings, even as it is supposed to improve communications. Who needs to interact with actual, living, breathing, flesh-and-blood people when computers will do it all for us?

Concerned about the excessive freedom which cell phones and other technologies afford our children. Freedoms that inevitably lead to the kind of disrespect for social order that results when children don't feel compelled to get permission from their parents.

I am young enough to appreciate the blessing of new technology. Yet old enough to know that blessings can also be curses.

And the thought occurs: this is what my parents must have felt every time they had to yell to get my attention as I listened to my Walk Man cassette player.

Lawnmowers – the Songbirds of Spring

Do you hear it?

I hear it. In fact, I bet that you and I are both part of it.

For anyone who loves spring as I do, the weekend sounds of lawn mowers, edge trimmers, hedge cutters, leaf blowers, fertilizer spreaders, core aerators, sod cutters, roto-tillers and other assorted lawn and garden implements are like a Saturday morning symphony.

Together, the cacophony is as beautiful and inspirational in its own way as just about anything this side of Mozart.

The sound embodies and announces spring, the best time of the year as far as I am concerned.

Glorious spring -- when vibrant, colorful life replaces drab death just when we seem to need it the most. Like a magnet it draws people out of their winter hovels to talk and mingle and work again. To share time and space and communal interests.

My wife and I tend proudly to what I think is some

impressive landscaping and a pretty cool little vegetable garden in the middle of our little hunk of suburbia.

Though I love the end result, I cannot take all of the credit for the beauty and bounty that those flowers and vegetables bring. That goes to Kellie and her mom, a certified master gardener. Together they have sculpted our little corner of the cul-de-sac into something colorful and fragrant from April to October.

It's taken four planting seasons to do, including some backbreaking labor on all of our parts – and little adjustments are still being made even now.

But the result is wonderful, especially on a late summer/early fall evening, sitting on the patio, reading a book, sipping a beer or an iced tea. Some people look to the heavens for proof of God. I look at my back yard.

My contribution comes largely from behind the lawnmower/wheelbarrow or whatever other implement must be pushed across the greens. Yes, I admit, I am a mule. But I am a mule who actually enjoys doing the work (don't tell my wife – it'll negate all the grousing I've done to foster my image as a curmudgeon.)

That's why I enjoy the sounds of all those gardening tools and machines so much. Their engines declare an aural pact between homeowners: "Let's make our little world as beautiful as we can," they say. "Your property is my property is their property is our property."

This phenomenon is somewhat unique to suburbia, I think.

Folks in the country are used to nature's wonders. They're surrounded by it, grow up with it. For them, dirt is dirt. The concrete jungle is their adventure.

But for those who grew up with asphalt under their feet, any little patch of topsoil becomes sacred.

It doesn't matter that the topsoil was scraped off the earth when the house was built and put back later, no more than six inches of real, life-sustaining dirt atop four feet of compacted clay, rocks and the builders' beer cans and assorted other garbage.

What matters is that this dirt, this grass, these trees – even though they're mere straplings, more big sticks than trees – all belong to me. I can stick my fingers in it. I can put seeds into it. I can shape it and mold it. I can do my very best to draw life from it

And if everything goes well, I can celebrate its contribution to nature's glory.

What's more, everyone benefits from such environmental effort.

There's the direct, tangible payoff – higher property values. But there's the more important, intangible effect, too: a sense of community, of shared interest, and beauty.

A beautiful yard makes for a beautiful neighborhood makes for a beautiful subdivision makes for a beautiful town makes for a beautiful…you get the idea.

With so much beauty at stake, what better alarm clock is there on a weekend morning, than a lawnmower?

Dear Dad, How About Some Snow?

I'm not usually very sentimental about snow.

You probably didn't know that about me, dad. I doubt it ever came up amid our discussions of such crucial issues as the fate of the Chicago Bears, our favorite John Wayne movies and the eternal debate over who made the best James Bond. (I still agree it was Sean Connery.)

The season's first snowfall is always nice, especially if it comes on or near Christmas. But, after the initial diamond-like sheen dulls, and tromping footprints destroy the baby skin-smooth veneer, there isn't much to like about snow.

It's messy, wet, cold and causes otherwise-expert drivers to conduct their vehicles like their heads are stored in the glove compartment.

Still, I've been thinking a lot about snow lately. Maybe it's because El Nino's warmer and sexier sister, La Nina, has seduced Mother Nature into giving us abnormally high temperatures. Maybe it's the holiday season.

In any case, I want snow this year, like the snow that

fell the day you died nearly 20 months ago, dad. That snow was so dense that my eyes struggled to remain open under its weight, before tears eventually closed them for good.

In that wistful mood, I am thinking about the time my brother and I said that we really wanted a snow mountain in the backyard.

I'm sure it was one of our many off-the-cuff childhood requests.

The romance of flying down a steep incline at breakneck speed, while steering to avoid the rocks, branches and roots that refuse to show any respect to the winter-hardened ground, puts many young bodies belly to wooden back on a sled. It must have fueled our young imaginations enough to prompt us to ask you to build us our very own hill.

Most parents – probably including me now -- would acknowledge such a request with a broad-faced, if slightly condescending promise to "see what we can do about that."

And of course, nothing would get done. How do you go about building a snow mountain, after all, in the flat-terrain of suburbia?

You did it, simply enough, by renting a snowplow.

It helped that, as a Will County Sheriff's deputy, you had "special" connections. But your connections alone didn't raise that mountain.

It's the rare father – it's the rare person – willing to take a child's foolish dream seriously and turn it into a glistening, frozen reality.

I admit I don't remember all the details. I was too

young then, and I'm getting too old now. But mom remembers for us, and for you.

One night, she recalls, after a full day's work, you brought that plow home and trucked bucket after bucket of snow from the nearby shopping center parking lot into our back yard.

Each load was another 15 minutes without sleep, each dump of the bucket another favor called in, until finally, near dawn, the parking lot was clean, and our yard had a new topography.

I don't think the diesel-fueled tractor rumbles gave us nocturnal hints about your activity. But I do remember waking that morning to find a veritable Mt. Hernandez on Joliet's East Side. And it was ours!

As I continue to stumble into and through my own fatherhood, I miss you terribly, dad.

We spent a lot of time in the oedipal overcast that shadows many fathers and their sons. We didn't talk much about our "real feelings" for each other. But gestures like the snow mountain said more about your love for us than any words ever could.

I know that you weren't perfect. Yet as Christmas approaches, I pray, more than ever, that I learn to emulate the one quality that even your worst shortcomings could never tarnish: the spirit of self-sacrifice needed to do whatever you could to protect your kids, help them and make them happy.

I don't know what kind of pull you have in heaven, dad, but I need your help again. I want snow this year, and lots of it. Because I want to build a mountain for my kids.

Too Small to Matter, Except to God

A week ago, I realized how small I am.

Not physically, though I am short. Not mentally or emotionally. Or even in stature or status. I am no Mike Royko, but I've done OK.

Rather, in significance.

And not just me. I realized how small everyone is who was not killed on September 11, 2001 by an airliner ripping into the World Trade Center or smashing into the Pentagon or crashing into a field.

The day of that terrible tragedy was my second day on a brand new job.

This is a big opportunity, this new job, for my family and me. Where it would lead I had no idea. But personally, professionally, financially, it was a huge stepping stone in the creek of my life.

Yet suddenly it meant nothing.

I sat there, listening to the radio, watching a television with coworkers so new I didn't even know most of their names, fielding updates from my wife and mother who were particularly glad that I no longer worked in the James R. Thompson Center in downtown Chicago, as I had only a week before.

In the face of devastation beyond anything I have ever seen – or anyone else, I suspect, who has not been at the business end of a gun in war – all of my accomplishments were reduced to particles. Smaller than the dust that turned southern Manhattan into a surreal, morbid cloud.

Because what can possibly compete or compare with that event?

As I write this, we do not know yet who did it, or why. We don't know how our country will respond.

Though, when my 8 and 6-year-old daughters, my love for whom defines and directs everything I do, asked if those responsible would be put in jail, I tried to calmly, rationally explain that no, our soldiers would probably kill them.

Have you ever spent a child's lifetime telling her that violence is wrong, that guns are bad and dangerous, that only God has the right to decide life and death, and then tried to explain that in this one case, death is an appropriate response?

Each week I comment about what it means to live in this area at this time. The good, the bad. The conflict, the tension. The people, the politics. These are important concerns in our world.

But in the real world, none of it matters.

Because in the real world, we, our problems, issues, challenges and achievements are small.

And yet there are some people whose all-too-human actions make them even smaller.

Of course, the people who would violently wrest control of an airplane and turn it into a guided missile to answer some voice in their heads that makes no sense to most of the rest of us.

People who would try to benefit from this tragedy. Gas stations spurred nightmarish visions of the 70s energy crisis, as cars lined up out onto the streets to fuel up and beat the rumors that gas would be $5 a gallon before nightfall.

"This is America," my brother said, referring to the capitalistic impulse that drives our economy. True enough. It's also immoral, unethical and sad.

But also because there are people and things bigger than us.

All the military, firefighters and cops willing to die -- despite every odd imaginable being stacked against them -- to try to build a wall between us and harm. And all of the everyday people who try to help when harm inevitably breaks through.

And God. Not the God of anger and vengeance and petty human politics that may end up being cited for the order to kill innocent people.

But the God who tells us that we can do nothing so bad that He cannot love us.

The God who begs, implores and teaches us to love each other the same way.

The God who promises us that we are more than carbon molecules randomly bumping together, and that there is something bigger, more meaningful, better for us.

A God who gives us hope – embodied in children, families and tomorrows – to comfort us, and carry us over our human smallness.

Saving Money, Saving Grace, Saving Face

I've spent most of my adult life not saying no.

Technically, "not saying no" is not the same as saying yes. But the bottom line is the same. We end up getting something that isn't necessarily needed. Rather, the procurement is the direct and often indefensible, illogical result of want.

This is a very American phenomenon. Humongous industries are built to serve the impulse buying that fuels the American economy. Every aspect of our society is strategically designed to service the god of Materialism.

Marketing results from and incorporates more scientific research than the space program. Those end caps at the front and back of each aisle and those special displays at the checkout counter, they aren't there by accident, you know.

Most commercials for national products cost more than the gross national product for most Third World countries.

And then there is credit. Unique to America, and

even more unique to the late 20th century, is the credit industry which lets people who don't have enough money buy whatever they want, as long as they promise to pay for it later. And in trade for that privilege (and for the opportunity to have something now! now! now!) we pay even more than what the original purchase would have cost.

As a result, fewer Americans than ever and especially people of my age group (I don't know what fancy name the media calls those of us in our early 40s) make any real effort to save money.

Why save, when we can get it NOW?

I'd like to say that I am a victim of this situation. I'd like to point a finger of blame at the marketing industry or the commercial hucksters or the credit companies.

But truth be told, I have been an active participant.

The fact is, every decision to buy something with any excess funds instead of saving that money; every lazy instinct to cash in whatever little savings we had to get over this rough patch or that tough spot rather than get a part-time job; every unchecked impulse (and there have been thousands over the years) to whip out a credit card to produce instant gratification; was a internal choice made, not an external punishment inflicted.

My wife and I were the poster children for the Reagan '80s. We were young. We worked hard, both holding down full and part-time jobs for the first several years of our marriage just to make ends meet.

But we also lived life. Mind you, we were not extravagant by any means. Rarely does a newspaper reporter who doesn't work at the Tribune Tower or swim nightly through a pile of Great Aunt Gertrude's inheritance live a life approaching extravagance. Still, we lived. And most of that living was done on credit cards.

Consequently, we spent almost everything we made on bills, and saved very little.

I didn't always like it. Spending money shreds my better sense like cheddar cheese against a grater. But I love being married…which is not to blame my wife for our shared life of spending, either.

Decisions made, even those made reluctantly, were made together.

We're trying to turn the ship, though it's harder to do with ones hands tied by the bonds of old(er) age. We've banked some hard-earned wisdom. Unfortunately, it can't buy us out of our past.

Now, however, we're noticing a quiet, but definite clucking noise. I'm pretty sure it's the sound of chickens coming to roost…

Our daughters earn – earn, not get – a monthly allowance. Plus, as young teens, they both make money in other ways, babysitting and such. (And of course, there's Grandpa, who frequently gives them money just because the sun came up. Being grandchildren -- nice gig, if you can get it…)

Their allowances go directly into savings accounts. But the conversations/debates/fights have already started about the money they "make" on their own.

Our own finances are our own business (pun intended.) The bigger question is how to teach our daughters the finer points, the glory and the beauty, of saving rather than spending, as they begin making their own money?

It's not as easy as saying "look at us." Unfortunately, for them and us, we haven't modeled the best example.

Probably, this is going to be one of those situations that require the old parental standby, usually reserved for one-time hippies, hell raisers and rabble-rousers of various other assorted types – "Do as I say, not as I do."

That's certainly not the best parental advice to give. Given our own financial indiscretions, though, it may be the best we can afford.

Santa 2008

Yes Virginia, there is a Santa Claus…

The modern Western media has long portrayed him as a jolly, fat man in a red, fur-lined suit wedged into a sleigh behind eight reindeer (or nine, depending on your position on the Rudolph controversy,) miraculously flying around the world, defying the space/time continuum and all laws of physics.

Yet, amid all of reality's many twists and turns, Santa in his truest form always takes a different form, depending on our own twisty, turn-y reality.

History bears this out. The Santa of Western culture evolved through numerous historical and cultural variations stemming from legends and traditions surrounding the 4th century figure of Saint Nicholas.

Interestingly, amid the different forms Santa has taken over the centuries, one constant theme among all of the myths is that he has especially cared for the downtrodden, poor and unhappy.

This year, there're a lot of downtrodden, poor and

unhappy people in our neighborhoods, communities and the world – perhaps more than usual given the state of the economy which has hit so many so hard.

So, I suspect, Santa will look a lot different for lots of people.

For some, Santa will look like an African American man. He will be delivering a big red bag of hope, vision, competence and intelligence to a world desperate for those gifts after eight years of getting lumps of intellectual, economical, cultural and political coal wrapped, deceptively, in shiny paper.

For some, he will look like a stranger delivering gift cards from the local grocery store, donated by others whom the recipient has never met. And a little extra thrown in to help pay for the rent and keep the heat and lights on. There may be few gifts under the tree, but at very least the kids won't be cold on Christmas morning.

Plenty of people will see Santa this year as the sweet, elderly lady at the pantry, handing over bags of food that was collected and donated by hundreds of school children as part of this event or that.

Many of those kids may never know whatever happened to that can of corn they brought to school at their teacher's urging. But in their little way, they, too will embody Santa this year.

Of course, Santa always wears the paramilitary uniform of the Salvation Army, ringing those bells and caring for the hundreds and thousands who desperately need the help of an army dedicated to spiritual salvation.

Likewise Santa will always look like the people who open the doors at the missions and shelters and agencies that care for those who otherwise cannot care for themselves – the homeless, the helpless, the abused.

And then there are the Santa's who cannot drive a sleigh.

The siblings who may drive you nuts most of the time, but always somehow come to the rescue when you're most in need, emotionally, physically, financially.

The children and nephews and nieces whose incessant chatter and unnatural energy normally push you to look for the nearest window ledge. Now that energy is seen for the gift it really is: unfettered joy and love for life. We could all, and always, use a little more of both.

The spouses who continue to love you in spite of who you have become. That person may be (and often is) quite different than who or what you, and they, thought you'd be.

The friends who may see every one of your faults yet ignore them -- though they hide in plain view, like the moon hanging around in the daytime sky.

Not to mention those on the other side of life's spectrum – the parents who lead by the quiet example of their own charity.

And the grandparents whose sheer existence affirms that we can survive most anything – recession, depression, war, traumatic loss, time -- with faith, perseverance, hard work, humor, perspective and a little sacrifice.

Even the pets whose constancy of affection and place remind that even the smallest gifts – a simple scratch of the belly, a few minutes throwing a ball – are worth everything.

The gifts that these Santa's will bring have nothing to do with helping the auto industry fix itself or bailing out banks or propping up the chain discount store's bottom line or even helping a favorite mom-and-pop shop survive until spring.

Santa is not a savior. He does not bring salvation. Just support. But part of Santa's magic, is that the gifts he brings are worth so much more than their actual cost.

And Santa will continue to appear to us just as we need him to be – the benevolent embodiment of the spirit of giving, kindness and love when such giving is needed the most.

Yes Virginia, the Santa's we see this year, amid recession and depression of all kinds, may look different than what we're used to.

But, like Santa's throughout history, and especially during difficult times, their greatest presents are gifts of the spirit and blessings for the soul.

Go Ahead! Bury Me Alive! Just Throw In My Books

Теперь я в суп!

That's Russian for, "I'm in the soup!"

I figured it would be good to brush up on my Russian, since I'll be immersed in the culture, if not the actual language, for the next several months.

No, I'm not going anywhere. Except very probably in my imagination. I will soon start reading Leo Tolstoy's classic novel "Anna Karenina."

My wife and I are both voracious readers.

She, though, is much more disciplined about her reading. She sets aside regular chunks of time, and doesn't let anything distract her as she plows through whatever tome is her focus du jour.

When she is reading, I could spontaneously combust. Twenty famished, salivating cannibals could be standing nearby with knives and forks at the ready. I could scream out to her for help…and she'd shush me. "Just a minute!" she would say, tersely. "I have a few more pages to go!"

Come to think of it, that could be a sign of her overall impression of me as much as her love of reading...

Anyway, the point is, not so, me.

I will read anything, anywhere, anytime. Books. Newspapers. Magazines. Cooking directions. Cereal boxes. The back of the air freshener can while enjoying my morning constitutional. Even major Russian novels.

But my reading habits make a blind, one-winged moth's flight path seem well planned.

That will have to change if I am going to make it through "Anna Karenina" and, if I survive, "War and Peace."

See, I may be disorganized in my reading, but I am maddeningly committed. I must finish whatever I start, no matter how boring or crudely crafted.

Words and ideas are so much my joy that I always hold out hope that the next sentence, next page, next chapter may be the turning point. The crossroads at which the writing finally explodes. The story begins to make sense. The mystery becomes clear.

I've given up on a book only once. It was Martin Buber's "I and Thou," a (supposed) classic of theology and philosophy. It very well may be. But at the time, as an antsy 20-something, the ideas were too thick, the writing too pretzel-twisted.

Tolstoy may present the same challenge. But it's a challenge I am excited to meet.

My reading covers a lot of ground. I tend to prefer fiction and lean toward classics and the better-reviewed modern writing.

This is not as snobbish as it may sound. I read both for the simple pleasure of a good story, and to experience good writing. I want to learn something as much as I want to escape into whatever new world the book conjures.

But I also love a good mystery. I've enjoyed several great biographies. And my avocation is scholarly theology. Or, as my family calls them, my "Jesus books." How the early Christian church rose from the blood-stained, tear-drenched dirt at Golgotha is a particular fascination of mine.

I've got hundreds of unread books. I tend to read both obsessively and compulsively. If I stumble onto a new author that I enjoy, I will buy everything I can by that author, and read it until I can't read it anymore.

I never borrow books. I must own them. They become like children to me. My wife insists she's going to put all of my unread books in the coffin with me. That's good.

I figure I'll be gone a long time, unless Houdini has finally figured out how to cross back over. Problem is, I've got so many books that she just may have to buy two coffins.

My greatest literary challenge is deciding what to read next. The last 100 pages of any book are always a particular misery, not usually because the book is ending, but because I start worrying about what will follow.

I solved this dilemma – ingeniously, I thought -- with "Daddy's Book Boxes."

Several years ago, I wrote the names of each of my books on individual paper strips and put them in a box, one each for my religious and non-religious libraries.

Now, when the time comes, one of my daughters will reach into Daddy's Book Boxes – alternating between my religious and secular collections -- and pick my next book. I know. The very definition of anal. But it sure eases my reading anxiety.

This time, "Anna Karenina" emerged, preceded by "The Case for Christ" by Lee Strobel. Then "War and Peace," if I live that long.

Heaven help me, but I do love reading.

Or, as they say in Russian, Небеса помогают мне, но я люблю чтение.

I Pledge Allegiance, to
(the Ideals Represented by) the Flag…

"I pledge allegiance…"

Indeed I do, but not to a piece of cloth.

I pledge allegiance to what that cloth represents.

As a lover of American democracy -- and as a person of strong spiritual faith – I am overjoyed at this recent and ongoing debate about the constitutionality of the words "under God" in the Pledge of Allegiance. It has caused so many people to finally practice and participate in what this country is really all about.

No, not the moronic rhetoric spouted lock-step by most of our idiot politicians responding to the recent California court decision that declared those two magic words unconstitutional. "Rush out and say the Pledge. It'll cure all the world's ills." Great thinking, folks.

And not the fascist "America -- love it or leave it" ramblings spat by extreme right-wing fanatics.

But rather, free speech, debate about great ideas and peaceable public dissent and demonstration.

Yes, that's what America is all about. That, and paradox. Self-contradiction. It's a beautiful mess of a system and I love it.

Indeed, our entire foundation is built on the premise that we are endowed with certain inalienable rights by "the creator." Our laws are a long-winded paraphrase of the Judeo-Christian vision of morality – thou shall not steal, kill, etc.

Our forefathers seem to have believed in God, and had no problem with the government including God in its own dealings. Yet they also said that the system itself could not tell anyone which God was the right God – or whether there was a God at all.

More paradox: our governing body is designed to create laws to help and protect us. Yet it is divided into three parts – the legislature, the courts and the presidency – that are specifically and purposely intended to check each other's work and limit each other's power to do their jobs.

It's amazing that the system works at all. Yet, somehow it does.

That's why I love this Pledge of Allegiance imbroglio. In its degree of ridiculousness, the depths of its paradox, it couldn't be more American.

Some people have argued that the Pledge never intended to honor or even mention God.

For example, Anna Quindlen, the wonderfully insightful columnist for Newsweek, wrote recently that the Pledge was written in 1892 for a magazine to honor Columbus Day, by a socialist who was forced out of his own church.

It was written, she says, as a vehicle to unite a country

divided by race, class and religion. "Under God" was not in the original.

"Under God" was inserted about 50 years ago during the McCarthy era at the prompting of the Knights of Columbus, a Catholic men's group, to counter "godless communism." That is, to say that those who believe in God are better than those who don't, Quindlen said. Not very uniting, is it?

On the other hand, others say that this country was founded on God's shoulders, so to speak. And that we are blessed, to whatever degree we believe ourselves to be, thanks to God's grace. So "under God" is perfectly appropriate.

Others, including Lance Morrow in a Time essay, say that though the phrase really doesn't belong in the Pledge, it shouldn't now be deleted given the politics of our time and the reinvigorating effect and value of patriotism.

And still others would agree with the Daily Southtown's terrific columnist Phil Kadner who wrote that the really important words in the Pledge aren't "under God," but rather "with liberty and justice for all."

Justice, Kadner wrote, implies tolerance for all, including those whose religious (and I would add social and philosophical) beliefs forbid them from taking an oath.

They're all right, which is very cool, if slightly confusing.

God – or whatever you call your higher power -- is a part of the American fabric.

People are right to support and pledge allegiance to something they believe in, especially in times of distress like we have now. Of course, politics inevitably feeds off of patriotism. Nothing we can do about that.

But Americans also have the brilliantly unique right to not say the Pledge. They can do so as a way of speaking against – and paradoxically for – their own government.

Even our own local nitwit politicians recognized this when they required all school students, now including high school students, to say the Pledge daily, but let them opt out if they or their parents object.

Free speech. Peaceable public dissent and demonstration. Debate of great ideas. God bless America.

Go ahead! Today, whether you believe in God or not, say the Pledge – or don't -- as a way to honor the very principles we pledge allegiance to.

Think what you want about me. But call me an American.

What Is More Patriotic Than Peace?

I am a patriot.

At least, I believe I am patriotic. But what I say next won't sound that way to some people, based on the kinds of letters that continue to appear in local newspapers, the comments that continue to be made, the rhetorical e-mail that flies on its little electronic wings to me.

I'll lay it on the line, clear as day, so that those who will take potshots can have all the time they need to sharpen your pencils:

I am opposed to the Iraqi war. Yet, I support our soldiers in this war with Iraq. And those statements are not, and do not have to be mutually exclusive.

Now in my apparently-feeble mind, it makes sense to hope for peace. And hoping for peace, to my warped way of thinking, means wanting our soldiers to be out of harm's way.

And right now, the harm they face is in Iraq, where they fight against a rag-tag military, many who themselves are fighting only at the end of a gun barrel pointed at their heads by their so-called leader.

I could be totally wrong. But I still do not see any justification for going to war with Iraq. I understand the idea of imminent danger. However I do not see imminent danger to America.

Still, our soldiers have earned every ounce of our deepest admiration.

Having been raised by a Vietnam veteran, having loved and respected a great uncle who was a WWII Purple Heart recipient, having known many fighting men and women, I understand the need for the military.

I deeply respect anyone who chooses to put on a military uniform, whether they end up being General Patton or Gomer Pyle, because the commitment is the same – the willingness to die for a belief.

I also understand that sometimes there is need for conflict if we are to protect our way of life.

See, the gist of our American system comes down to two uniquely American, essential, and essentially intertwined rights: to choose those who will govern us, and to criticize those who will govern us. Without both of those rights, America is no better than any slag heap, third rate excuse for a country anywhere in the world.

It's like the old joke comparing humans to the rest of the animal kingdom: by all measures, we should be dung between elephants' toes. Other animals are bigger, faster, stronger, better able to survive in the wild.

But God gave us two things: intellect, and opposable thumbs. With those tools, we have climbed to the top of the food chain.

America is much the same.

Without the vote and the ability to tell our leaders what we think of them, what are we? Nothing special very special, that's for sure.

Other countries have elections, including Iraq. Saddam Hussein was recently "re-elected" with nearly 100 percent of the vote. But anyone who dares speak out against him not-so-mysteriously disappears.

That doesn't happen in America. Here, we have the right to protest our government. It's one of several rights that make us unique in the history of mankind. So comments chastising people for opposing this war infuriate me.

If indeed our soldiers are fighting to protect our American way of life, then they are fighting precisely for our right to criticize this war. And to protest our government. And to burn the American flag. And to not say the Pledge of Allegiance -- with or without "under God" -- if we so choose.

And to criticize those who criticize. It's a vicious, self-contradicting, maddening loop, I know, but there is nothing more American. I may not like or agree with what you are saying, but I defend your right to say it. You owe me, and everyone like me, the same courtesy.

Recently this controversy reached the heights of ridiculousness in a movie ad.

The producers of the new pre-teen film "What a Girl Wants," with Nickelodeon star Amanda Bynes, changed the original ad to remove an image of Bynes making the "peace" sign with her hand. They wanted to avoid making any political statement.

Peace is now a political statement?

No. Peace is what we should all be after if indeed we

support our soldiers. And if that means criticizing our government to get it, so be it. Because only peace will bring our fighting men and women home safely.

Nothing is more American, or patriotic.

Impatient for Asparagus

We have asparagus!

The tasty, tall green stalk is one of my favorite vegetables. I love it no matter how it is prepared: roasted, cooked in the microwave, raw in salads, with melted fancy-shmancy cheese on top.

Asparagus is one of my favorites because it's a little eating escapade all by itself. The difference in texture and taste from the smooth stem to the crunchy head... mmm!

It's so good, in fact, that I could eat it right out of the garden.

And now, finally, I can!

Until recently, we had to buy our asparagus at the grocery store. But, gladly, no more.

Because two weeks ago, we cut the first real-live asparagus stalks from our own garden. And it took only two years to get them!

See, asparagus plants must bloom and die for at least two full planting seasons before they will produce anything worth eating. This spring marked the beginning of the third season. And now, after much careful cultivation, voila! One less thing for which we have to run to the store.

Much as I love the veggie's flavor though, our asparagus adventure has produced something even greater: patience.

Well, not completely. Patience is always in short supply in my personal storehouse of virtues.

But, knowing how much I love it, longed for it, and worked for its eventual harvest, the anticipation of the asparagus's eventual arrival was a constant reminder that the best things in life are worth waiting for.

Patience is indeed a gift. Not one that I actually can claim, mind you, but one I certainly admire and aspire to.

I've never been willing to wait for much of anything.

That guy driving too closely behind you, honking and dashing to your left to try to pass, even though you're driving the speed limit? That's me.

The knucklehead yelling at the computer because it's too slow – though simultaneously recognizing that the world spins about a million miles faster because of same said computer – me again, guilty as charged.

Waiting for any kind of package, from the simplest used CD from Amazon.com, to a paycheck, to arrive in the mail drives me bonkers.

That the hinge on the mailbox door hasn't died from exhaustion from me checking for packages, is a testament to the craftsmanship of whoever makes mailbox door hinges.

My calm wife, so often the bemused if not irritated witness to this (yet another) character flaw, tries to set me straight.

"Don't worry," she counsels. "Slow down. It (whatever "it" is) will get here soon enough."

To which I think, with all the love and admiration and respect a spouse can muster in the face of such obvious and keen logic, "What do you mean, 'Soon enough'?! 'Soon enough' is not as soon as 'now', which is really all I want. Is 'NOW' so much to ask?"

And in those rare times when my wife cannot break me of my addiction to immediacy, God, in some kind of clever disguise, steps in and gently but firmly slaps me upside the head.

Traffic will suddenly converge, forcing me to slow down, back away from the bumper of the driver in front of me, and resume a safer, saner distance and speed.

And then, a traffic cop will appear radar gun in hand, proving that God has a sense of humor -- and that He's in cahoots with my wife.

Or the check will come in the mail just as I am about to dial the "lost check" line and yell mercilessly at whoever answers the phone, knowing full well that they've likely got nothing to do with the seeming delay.

And now, my latest encouragement and reminder to not rush everything, just popped out of the ground.

Asparagus may seem like an odd messenger for God. Until you remember that He once spoke to Moses from inside a burning bush. Then it doesn't seem so strange that He might take on the form of a green stalky vegetable to impart some wisdom to me.

Slow down. Wait. Everything will happen in due

time, when it's supposed to. Be patient. There's too much good in life to blow by just to get to the mall 38 seconds sooner.

Now, I must go sample some of our very own garden-grown asparagus. I just cannot wait another minute!

Ok, so I still have some work to do with this "patience" thing…

"Partying" Is Not Always Good

Which is worse?

That one side would do it, or that the other would do it, too, given the chance?

Recently, right-wing radio blowhard Rush Limbaugh openly, boisterously and maliciously said he wishes and hopes that President Obama fails.

After being chastised by the media – and even some Republicans – Limbaugh clarified. He compared his feelings about Obama to his feelings about the Super Bowl.

He is a fan of the Pittsburgh Steelers, Limbaugh said. Watching the game, he wished and hoped that the Arizona Cardinals and quarterback Kurt Warner would fail, Limbaugh said.

Limbaugh blathered on to his salivating sycophants that he believes that the economy will run better if left entirely to the private sector, that if rich people are left alone, all will be well with the world again, blah, blah, blah…

Spoken like a true multi-millionaire who hasn't done anything more important than yell into a microphone and call for tougher drug abuse policies – while abusing the pain killer oxycontin.

And for Limbaugh to compare his comments about President Obama to a football game is insulting to every American, from Warren Buffet and Bill Gates to the poorest migrant worker. We are talking about the country's economic health, its very survival. Not a bet made over nachos and beer.

Oh, and then of course, following a conservative/right wing agenda obviously worked so well for the last eight years.

Don't tell me that the housing collapse was caused solely by Democratic policies allowing poor people to borrow money that they couldn't pay back. Yes, that was a part of it, for sure.

But I didn't see many banks, especially the mega-giants, turning away any of that extremely profitably business, concerned about the risks that poor people were taking with their livelihoods, homes and futures.

Nope, they found plenty of ways to squeeze very real profits out of pretend money and schemes so complex even the bankers were confused.

Both Republicans and Democrats share blame for creating a system that allowed and encouraged all of this to happen.

But in the end, the blame must fall just a little bit more on the Republicans because their man was president. He was the de-facto leader of the party and the leader indeed of the country. He set the tone. He set the bar.

Yes, Congress makes the laws, and President Bush

battled a Democratic-controlled Congress through part of his presidency.

But the president has the power of the bully pulpit. He drives the national car, so to speak. Everything flows from his leadership, or lack of it. Frankly, had Bush been a better president, more Republicans might have been elected to Congress to support his policies.

Likewise, President Obama will be held responsible – and get credit -- for whatever happens on his watch. Fair is fair. It comes with the office.

I am not now, nor was I ever a fan of George W. Bush. Yet, I never wished for him to fail.

He did fail, to be sure. But I always hoped that somewhere, sometime during his presidency he would have gotten something right. Sadly that didn't happen. Still I wish it had, because his success would have been our success.

Put another way that Republicans should recognize and appreciate, whatever the president does "trickles down" to the rest of us.

Every American has a right to his or her opinion. And certainly there are viable, important differences in approach between liberals and conservatives.

Yet, why would anyone plainly wish for the president to fail if it means, as it does now, that the entire country could also flounder as a result of said failure?

But the sad, divisive and destructive reality – fueled by American politics, American media and human nature -- is that many people from both sides of the aisle do exactly this.

Republicans and Democrats alike align themselves so deeply with their political ideologies; they are so indebted to their political sponsors that they cannot allow themselves to be more than just Republicans or Democrats.

Clearly and obviously, the refusal by every single Republican Congressperson to support the economic stimulus package was a political gesture. They cared more about their political ideology than they did about their own constituents.

Yet, Democrats would have done the exact same thing if John McCain had been elected and crafted his own economic rescue plan. Sad, sad, sad.

We may disagree about a lot of things when it comes to politics. But in this, President Obama was exactly right:

The stakes are too high for our elected officials to continue fighting to see who can puff out their chest more, who can spit further, who can yell louder. It is time for our elected officials at every level, of every persuasion, to set politics aside and work together.

America is about more than party politics. America is, first and foremost, about Americans.

On the Next "Oprah" -- Men Who Love Barbie

Suddenly, I stopped laughing.

The radio program I had been listening to one recent Sunday morning had gone in an instant from amusing to amazing. Not in a "this is so cool" sense of amazing, but in an "I can't believe anyone really feels this way."

The show, a usually-terrific radio program called "Satellite Sisters," featured a Seattle step-mom who said she was incredibly bored by and uninterested in her stepsons' and her husband's love for baseball.

So put off she was, that she could not bring herself to attend one more little league game or Mariners pro baseball contest, she told the program hosts in her best/worst "I-am-so-burdened-my-world-has-lost-its-focus" tone.

That's when my pleasure turned into anger.

Any parent who cannot at least pretend to like his or her children's interests or activities for the simple yet profound purpose of supporting and loving the kids, should turn in his or her Parenting Club card immediately. They don't deserve to have children.

In fact, if someone could develop a pre-pregnancy test to determine if a woman absolutely cannot get in line with football/karate/little league/paintball or some other typical-boy activity; or a man cannot get behind Barbie/gymnastics/ballet/art classes or some other typical-girl to-do, maybe then those prospective parents can be fixed beforehand and save everyone a little trouble.

Because learning to love what your children love, your own interests aside, is absolutely the least – and the most --that you can do for them.

Them is some tough words, I know. Fightin' words to some. But I mean every one of them. Because I have lived them.

My own mother, before my brothers and I joined a private league football club, never saw a pigskin that she didn't think should have been cooked or pickled. But, she was a woman in a world of men – three boys and a husband. And her men all played and loved football.

That meant learning the joys of sitting outdoors on hard metal or wooden bleachers (or folding chairs or blankets on the ground, as some of the fields didn't have bleachers) in weather unfit for man, beast or anyone not wearing 40 pounds of padding.

It meant learning enough of the intricacies of a very intricate game, sometimes unassisted (Dad was often on the sidelines helping coach or videotaping the game) to understand why people were cheering for their sons.

It meant – burden of all burdens – eventually coming to love the Chicago Bears in the Abe Gibron/Neal

Armstrong eras, not too unlike the Dave Wannstedt/ Dick Jauron eras.

It meant sacrifice.

My dad did the same thing, sitting through years of band concerts, fall plays and spring musicals. (Ok, he might have dozed through some of those, but at least he got himself sufficiently debriefed so that he could talk about them later.)

And I, a male island in a sea of women – the Bizarro World version of my mom -- am doing it now with my daughters.

Personally, I have no use for Barbie.

With no visible means of support, spousal or personal, I think Barbie has been living off of Ken (or maybe some other form of income) for 50 years now and presents a way-bad image for the "Grrrll Power"-ed daughters of the third millennium. But, my daughters, like all their peers, have fallen into the Barbie trap. So, cautiously, we go along.

Likewise I had lots of other stuff to do all those Saturday and Sunday mornings than to cart my eldest off to dance class.

A fan of Miles Davis, Tony Bennett, James Cotton, James Brown, Prince, KISS and Bob Dylan, I harbor no particular love for The Backstreet Boys or 'N Sync. And yet, my wife and I practically memorized their CD's (which aren't half bad, truth be told.)

Not to mention all the talk about clothes, makeup, Disney princesses, Power Puff Girls, slumber parties and (yes, it's starting already) BOYS…

I'm no saint. Sometimes, such "girl" stuff bores me

to tears. But it interests them, so I go along. That's what parents do.

And if anyone wants to argue about it, they can meet me at high noon in the American Girl store.

A Great Day for Art, Attitude, and Olivia

September 11 will always and forever be a happy day for me.

That sounds strange to most people, understandably, given the sad events now inextricably associated with the date.

But I don't say it to shock or awe. Rather the day will be – is -- special because it is our youngest daughter's birthday – and more so this year because it is her golden birthday.

Ever since the attack, Olivia has had to endure the mostly-innocent, yet still-pointed questions and comments about her birthday that only kids can pose -- along the lines that the day is somehow cursed, as is she, by extension.

But as we've told her, she came along six years before the tragic events that now identify September 11. So it has always been a special day –and for much happier reasons – for us.

Olivia was our planned child.

My wife insists that our eldest daughter, Emma, was

an accident, the result of her forgetting to take her birth control during a very busy time in our young marriage. I figured my wife just figured it was time and didn't bother to tell me. I no longer debate the point. Knowing when to give up an argument is the better part of valor in marriage.

Either way, the clock was now ticking, pun intended.

We believed that siblings born closer together (eventually) develop tighter bonds. So we decided to have our second child as soon as possible.

Circumstances dictated a planned C-section delivery. So we were able to literally schedule Olivia's birth – in the hospital by 6 a.m., have the baby by 8 a.m., dad back at the office by 1 p.m. at the latest.

Olivia has been a child of just such precision ever since.

She is very literal, making it frustrating sometimes to do anything that requires the suspension of disbelief or the application of metaphor or symbolism.

Watching movies or television programs, listening to certain songs, etc. can become a chore as we have to explain that the actors are not the characters, or that the singer may not have really done all the things that the lyrics suggest.

And she loves math, which can be particularly and especially vexing for a writer-father whose life is dominated by the other side of his brain.

Still, Olivia is one of the most creative people I've met.

She has started more unique businesses than any five Donald Trumps – painting and selling rocks, making and selling origami animals, decorating and selling wooden plant stakes, creating and selling homemade salad dressing, cleaning cars for a fee. (The "selling" is key – like all entrepreneurs, this kid likes the smell of money…)

Likewise Olivia loves art. She has taken up painting and drawing of every kind – water colors, tempura, chalk, pencils, ceramic snowmen and fish and holiday ornaments with her great aunt.

Then like a water bug flitting across the pond of art, she jumped to origami. Our home looked like a paper factory hit by a bomb. Then this past spring, after watching the Patrick Swayze vehicle "Ghost," she fell in love with clay, and took a park district pottery course.

Like most parents my wife and I have often marveled at the differences in our kids' personalities. And like most parents, we're often baffled. We raise them the same, we love them the same, we feed them the same, etc.

Yet they turn out so different.

Perhaps the reason (at least partly) lies in their own relationship. Being second-born often creates challenges that first-borns don't understand.

And it probably didn't help that our eldest, upon meeting her baby sister for the first time, identified her with the only living thing she'd met that was smaller than her – a dog.

As she saw her mom holding the baby, our first-born said, "Can I pet it?" Not "her," but "it."

Like all second children Olivia has worked ever since to carve her niche in our family in her own way. Whereas her sister's presence is known by default of being first, Olivia has had to stake her claim in life through sheer confidence.

She is, if only in her own mind, right as rain, in every decision she makes, no matter how far off the beaten path. Attitudinally, she can be 10 pounds of attitude in a five pound bag. Sometimes that's a good thing. Other times, it's enough to drive a saint to sin.

But that can-do attitude, that confidence, that charisma, that vim and vinegar, has already brought her a long way. And, I suspect, it will carry her through life in ways that those who doubt themselves can only envy.

So on her special day, we wish Olivia a happy birthday. You are very special to us, and for more than just the date of your birth.

A Thursday Closer

For a country built on the ideal of inclusion, America excludes a lot of people.

America has a long history of pushing people out, shoving them back, holding them down with a fat, fascist foot across the throat.

It doesn't matter if the "other people" were here first -- the Native Americans – or were dragged here in chains – African Americans.

This country has made an art of hating and belittling anyone different than the arbitrary "norm", whether the norm is based on race, language, religion, sexual orientation, gender, age, financial status, intellectual acumen or political affiliation.

Pick your "ism". Racism, age-ism, gender-ism. Our country, from sea to shining sea, from corner to corner, has practiced and endorsed it, or likely will before we draw our last breath.

Of course, the ironic and redeeming fact is that the "norm" changes generation to generation, year to year, sometimes day to day. Good. Perhaps one day we'll simply run out of inconsequential things to divide us and reasons hate each other.

That's why I, and many others, got choked up last Thursday.

When Barack Obama accepted the Democratic party's nomination for president of these here United States on August 28, 2008, a wall, metaphoric and symbolic, but as real as the tens of thousands of people filling that football stadium, crumbled right there on national television.

And I, an aging, suburban white guy, snuffled back tears of joyful pride.

Not to make too much of it, but Obama's nomination is one of the most significant developments in this country's deceptively-young history. (It only feels like America has been around forever, because we've done such a good job of making ourselves the center of the universe.)

Nominating an African American to the presidency is not as big as the Revolutionary War from which the country was born. Nor as the Civil War which first divided, then forcefully reunited the country. Nor, perhaps, even as the Civil Rights movement which gave an entire class of people voice and place.

But it connects the dots between those three defining events by culminating their purpose and promise – to ensure certain inalienable rights for all people. Including, most especially, the rights of equality and freedom.

We tend to forget this, because Americans tend to forget about God except when it's expedient -- Sundays, certain holidays, and right-wing political rallies.

But freedom and equality are God-given. But we've

done our human darned-est to deny them to our brothers and sisters since the day America spluttered to life at the hands of a group of men seeking – irony of ironies – religious freedom and political equality.

Now comes Barack Obama.

Born of a multiracial couple, raised in a fatherless home, Obama has become a man of intelligence, eloquence and grace. Quite a contrast to the Current Occupant...

I believe, in a heart filled with faith in a God who celebrates all of His creation, that Obama will be the next American president. And a great one.

Certainly not because of the color of his skin. There will be those who will blame every miscue, every mistake, every misjudgment on his African American blood (and there will be mistakes, because he is, still, human.)

Rather, he will be a great president because Obama knows what it means to actually, you know, work for a living. To survive without privilege. To rise to the height of heights of his own volition and hard work, not riding the coattails of his family's money and name.

He has carried crosses that none of his predecessors could even imagine, much less understand.

The weight of those burdens has already shaped him into a different kind of man and leader. A better leader, because he can truly identify with those who have been capriciously kicked to society's curb.

Yet another old, rich white man is not going to be able to bring this level of humanity to the White House.

None of which is to say that he will solve all of the country's problems, much less the world's.

No one person should be blamed for everything that's

wrong. Nor should any individual get credit for everything that's right. American democracy is strategically and specifically designed to prevent individuals from gaining just that kind of power.

Nor will President Obama solve racism.

Indeed, the very fact that we're celebrating Obama as the first African American presidential nominee is itself a form of racism.

Indeed, racism won't be the dinosaur it deserves and needs to be until we no longer frame achievement by skin color. Remember? Dr. King dreamed of a nation in which his "four little children will one day …be judged by…the content of their character."

We're not quite there yet. But we are one Thursday closer.

Memory's Madhouse of Mirrors

It was so much smaller than I remembered.

Last week I found myself on the far east side of Joliet for a work function. So I took a few minutes to swing through the neighborhood where I grew up. A quick dash down Memory Lane, then back to the daily grind.

Not much had changed from the time I lived there, from the ages of 3 to 13.

The neighborhood was, and is, gritty, urban, plain. And in its own way, beautiful.

It is still a blue collar bastion of old-fashioned houses, home to young people of all varieties at the start of life and old people nearing the end, tucked behind an old shopping center.

The center used to be anchored by a Zayre's – a discount department store that was kind of a forerunner to today's Wal-Mart – and a Kroger grocery. In its day, it was something of a big deal.

Our house fronted the center's back. This was long before municipalities thought it prudent to require developers to put fences and berms and walls between their strip malls and adjacent houses. We spent countless hours cavorting in the loading areas across the street. That concrete and blacktop was our playground.

Bordering the neighborhood on the other side is a street leading to downtown Joliet, with a few new stores. Nothing fancy. Just several blocks of restaurants, bars and businesses, some with hand-lettered signs in the windows advertising to customers who sometimes have to work an extra job to edge into the "middle class" income bracket.

Some vacant lots that existed when I lived in the area were now grassed over. Including the one just out of our mom's line of sight, where my brother Tim would imitate Evel Knievel.

He'd jump his bike over ramps, flying fearlessly, higher and farther each time. He had much more success than Evel. At least, he broke fewer bones. I, never as crazy-brave as Tim, would set up the ramps, cheer and help him get back home in one piece.

Then I drove up the gravel alley that separated the two rows of houses that more or less defined our neighborhood. With a twinge of excitement, I looked for the back of the home that formed so much of my life.

But it was gone.

At least, what I remembered was gone.

In my mind, the house itself was huge.

Now it looked so tiny. Missing was the "shed" that my dad built – really a glorified overhang extending from the house underneath the second-story porch. I wouldn't have had my worst enemy lean against the walls of that thing. Dad wasn't much of a handyman.

And the lilac bushes that my parents planted that

made the front porch area smell like heaven's perfume outlet. Also gone.

Bigger yet in my memory was the back yard, where we played countless games of baseball and football.

The field of play was defined by the brick wall separating our group of houses from an adjacent cement factory; mom's vegetable garden; the raised concrete slab that was the neighbor's driveway; and, either our own pool or the house belonging to our Aunt Lil, who lived next door. The actual layout depended on what game we were playing.

Not to mention the steel clothesline pole in the middle of our field. There were unique consequences – namely, a painful headache and possible broken nose – for violating that special boundary.

And of course, Chico's pit.

Chico was Aunt Lil's vicious, slobbering, killer, blood-dripping-from-his-teeth black mutt of a dog. He lived in a doghouse tucked between the corner of her yard and her neighbor's chain link fence.

Chico would charge and snap and snarl and growl at anything. If, God forbid, a ball rolled into the pit – the dirt area he carved within the radius of his leash -- the game was over. Unless Aunt Lil or our cousin Dolores were home. They were the only ones who could enter Chico's pit and come out with all limbs intact.

Stopping my car, I stared. It all rushed back. And almost as quickly, rushed away.

I saw what was right in front of me. And what was behind me. In my mind, that yard had been as big as Soldier Field. Certainly the biggest in the neighborhood.

The house was gigantic. A two story, four-bedroom castle.

But now both looked so small.

Perspective, of course, accounts for some of the difference. As a child, everything looks bigger. And I was witnessing the usual consequences from generations of time and transition.

But even understanding those facts didn't ease the awkward feeling caused by seeing my past in a way that didn't fit. Memory is a funny thing, the way it distorts and stretches and re-orders life.

This was not my house anymore. Not my yard. Not my neighborhood. It's certainly a part of who I was, but not who I am.

I am not especially sentimental. I've gone to only two reunions. I don't think high school or college were the "best years of my life," as many people predicted. The present has always been more to my liking.

I looked for a few seconds more, and then drove away.

What's In A Name?

Thirteen, maybe 14, I had felt the slur's sting before.

"I don't want you talking to that spick anymore," I heard the woman say from the background as I talked on the telephone to her daughter, one of my junior high school girlfriends.

Twenty years later, I don't remember what my girlfriend said at the time. Probably something like, "Don't mind her." But I did mind.

It wasn't the word itself that was so shocking. Rather it was the relationship between the woman and myself.

There was none.

This woman had never met, talked to or seen me. She couldn't have known that I was adopted. My last name is Mexican, but my blood isn't. I was as Anglo as her.

What bothered me then, was that this mother, responsible for shaping her child's mind, had identified and judged me based on nothing more substantial than my last name.

What bothers me now, with two kids of my own is

the possibility that 20 years of personal racial activism and political correctness hasn't done as much as thought or hoped to eradicate the hateful, ignorant racism that yields attitudes like that woman's.

My name is my personal paradox. I have learned to love my unique, if ironic racial status. But I worry about how society will view and treat my daughters, twice removed from the bloodline that shapes their identity.

I've met racism in all its forms.

Like most minorities, I am deeply offended by the misinformed, shortsighted thinking that trivializes a person because of something as uncontrollable and circumstantial as skin color, gender or ethnicity.

Don't be fooled by my pale pigment. I am as much a minority as anyone. In fact, my "pseudo ethnicity" may put me even more in the social margin than most other traditional minorities, including even children born of mixed marriages.

I am actually something of a European "mutt," more German than anything else.

Still, I proudly consider myself part Mexican.

When people look at me askance, wondering why my skin color doesn't match my moniker, I say I am Mexican by background, not by blood; by culture, not corpuscle.

With my father's name came the welcome gift of his world. I grew up surrounded by my paternal family.

I can't speak as much Spanish as I could or should – I got through two years of high school Spanish through the grace of God and the help of a girlfriend. Still, I will eagerly endorse bilingual classes for my children as a step toward a more successful future for them.

I know the spicy joy of real Mexican food. I love the

romantic rhythms of Latino music of all derivations. I recently started adding Latino literature to my library.

In a way, I am the American ideal – a true cultural melting pot, polished by and reflecting several distinct influences.

But there are two sides to each Peso.

Certainly, I have known the disgusted dismissal common to folks who look, speak or live differently than the "majority." But I have also experienced a kind of reverse racism that both benefited and offended me.

Six months into my first post-college job, I learned that my employers falsely assumed I spoke Spanish. I never said I did, and my employer never asked. But when they learned as much, they were upset, I was told.

I did a good job. But I could never quite escape the suspicion that some people felt I was hired for some reason other than my abilities.

As well, I have routinely endured the water cooler racism – ethnic slurs and jokes -- common in most workplaces. I am always astounded that people would say such things around me, knowing my name. They must assume that, because I look like them, I think like them and won't mind their comments.

"I may not have his blood," I think silently, incensed by their insensitivity, "but I am still my father's son." Yet, I am ashamed to admit that I rarely spoke up to object to such behavior.

Well down the road of adulthood, I have changed a bit. I am optimistic enough to think the world has changed with me. But I know, change comes slowly, when it comes at all.

Newsweek magazine recently reported that Latinos

will be the country's largest minority group by 2050. I believe that such a cultural shift will add another exciting flavor to the American Pie.

But greater numbers of course bring greater position and power. Inevitably, that will cause jealousy and resentment among those losing clout and control.

I fear that as a result, my girls will be held accountable for something they had no control over, and begrudge something they should boast about. Something which, more than not, has been a gold star on the chart of my life – something which, as it does for me, makes them special.

That would be terribly sad. Like most young children, my girls don't yet know racism of any kind, and I hope they never do.

Because they love the world regardless of its ethnicity, color or name.

Performing the Music of Life

I am a musician.

That's one of the things I used to say to describe myself. Right up until the recent broadcast of Bruce Springsteen in concert.

I played sax, and a handful of times I performed in a couple of bands at small events. No matter the size of the venue or the crowd, there was a real thrill to those performances.

The joy of making music, of performing, of making people feel whatever it was that we, the musicians, felt, through the energy and voice of the music. There's a real power in music that is seductive and addictive, both.

That same power was palpable even through a small television screen as Springsteen and the E Street Band tore through their set.

As was the audience there, thousands strong, I was moved to tears of sadness and joy and exaltation as Bruce sang about September 11, and good friends, and loved ones.

And when he ended with "Dancing in the Dark," a chestnut from his 1980's heyday, literally jumping around the stage, only my fear of knocking over furniture kept me from jumping around the living room with him.

That's when it hit me.

I am not a musician anymore.

I have not played that saxophone or any other instrument in years. I have not performed in front of an audience in more than a decade -- save several church functions in which I acted and passably sang.

A twinge of regret hit me. Not because this came as any surprise. I know that my fingers haven't caressed an instrument in years.

But rather, because I had willingly let go of a part of me. I chose to not continue playing music, something that was precious to me and a part of my identity.

I traded away the excitement of performing and playing and the limelight -- such as it was in bars or at weddings. I had traded away something of myself.

And, as I stood there alone in my house on a Saturday morning, ironing my daughters' clothes while they spent the weekend with their grandparents and my wife was at work, I wondered, what had I gotten in return?

Then, as so often happens, reality slapped me in the face. Bruce broke into another song called "Mary's Place," a simple tune that directly and bluntly speaks to the power of family and friends and the love that brings and keeps us together.

What had I gotten in return?

I got real life. The greatest adventure of all.

I got a wonderful wife, who has been my audience of one for more than 18 years. She has cheered for me in every endeavor, even when I did stuff that would embarrass even the staunchest supporter.

She has encouraged me in every folly I pursue. And she has hoisted me up when I have fallen with love, grace and the occasional (and occasionally necessary) kick in the pants. She is not perfect, nor am I. But she is much more the person I want to be than I am.

I got two intelligent, beautiful, loving, caring, adventurous, witty children. They are my daily proof of God.

Their smiles convey His love for me. Every tear is another chance for me to return some of that love. I often fail miserably as a dad, but they continue to give me chance after chance to do better.

I got a wonderful family -- a remarkable mother-in-law who was Martha Stewart before Martha was Martha (and way before Martha was in trouble.) A father-in-law who in some ways has been a better father to me than my own dad was.

I got a sister-in-law and aunt-in-law, both extraordinary single women who prove what I hope my daughters learn early and remember forever -- that men are not required for success or happiness.

I got a wagon full of experiences ranging from the exceptionally unexceptional -- diapers and fever -- to the quietly extraordinary -- seeing each of my babies wake up the next morning; watching them become young women.

This is a celebration, not a lament. I truly wish that everyone would be able to share it.

Instead of the life of a musician, I got the music of life. Flowing in and around and through me, every second of every minute of every day.

I am a musician.

Who's Cooler? Keith and Mick? Paul and John? Mom and Dad!

The Stones are all about sex.

The statement – more complicated than it seems -- was my answer to a simple question from my 15-year-old daughter.

Both she and her 12 ½-year-old sister in recent months have been doing what most teens do. No, not that. Well, if they are doing that, I don't know about it. Nor do I want to.

Rather, my girls, as young teens, are finally discovering their parents' music. And, – wow, what a concept – appreciating it.

This phenomenon is not uncommon. I saw it all the time when I worked as a teen in a music store.

Usually it was the Beatles. As they realized that there was more to life than the bubble gum pop that they'd been fed, kids would come in the store to buy "Rubber Soul" or one of the revolutionary group's landmark recordings that exploded musical boundaries.

Now my own children are doing the same. As they expand their minds, cultural horizons and Ipods, my girls are constantly looking for new music.

My wife and I are both voracious readers and enjoy a wide range of styles.

Likewise with our music. We have hundreds of CDs, tapes and yes, even albums and 45s – yes, I am that old. Our tastes span the musical globe from country (mostly my wife, though I like it, too) to R&B, blues and jazz (more to my tastes.)

And of course, lots of rock and roll from nearly every decade and generation.

Our family loves to talk. Other people, observing the way we interact with our kids, have suggested that us actually "talking together" is only slightly less strange than the fact that we actually like each other and enjoy spending time together. Whatever. Their loss…

Anyway, both of our kids are comfortable conversationalists. So it came as no surprise when, recently, our eldest asked me who was better – the Beatles, or the Rolling Stones.

No surprise. But certainly a pleasant opportunity for Dad to prove that he is, as he always says, omnipotent and omniscient, very nearly perfect and an expert on everything!

Or, at very least, it was a chance to talk a bit about music predating 1995.

The question isn't which is better, I explained. Because both were the best at what they did. But what they did was different.

The Beatles redefined pop music. Not once, but numerous times in significant ways. Their fingerprints are all over everything that came after them, even today, nearly 40 years after they split.

The Beatles were many things to many people. But they were not rock and roll. They were about the business of making great music.

The Rolling Stones were about the business of making rock and roll. True rock and roll – as it was in the beginning, is now and ever shall be – is about sex. Down and dirty, lascivious and loud. The Stones could have sung the phone book, and it would have sounded sexy and naughty.

Through movies and television programs, my girls have also stumbled onto R&B and the blues. Once, they heard Raven Symone, former child star of the "Cosby Show" and 'tween-teen star of her own show on the Disney Channel, singing "Superstition."

I'll never forget the "You're-too-old,-you-can't possibly-know-about-anything-this-cool" look on their faces when they told me about Raven's "new" song.

I couldn't contain my delight when I told them that not only did I know about "Superstition," but that I had two completely different versions of the same song. The original, by Stevie Wonder, and Texas blues legend Stevie Ray Vaughn's electrified work-up.

"Hah!" I thought. "Finally, they will come to understand that we do actually know what we're talking about, and that we are indeed cool!"

We're still working on the "cool" part.

But the girls have since agreed that their mom and I do know our music. Now, whenever they hear a song that they don't know, they immediately turn to us. "Do you have that one?" they will ask. More often than not, the answer is yes.

Which is a testament both to the fact that we really love music and value its place both in our lives as thoughtful, informed and intelligent people; and that most current music isn't good enough to sell movies and television shows.

They understand that Ray Charles was, truly, brilliant. And that Led Zeppelin was the prototype heavy metal band.

I've explained how James Brown, through his musical firepower and incredible star power gained serious political power. He single-handedly showed an entire people how to rise above the fray, by being proud of who they were.

And that what Bob Dylan was singing was more important than his actual singing – but that his voice and music were equally important parts of a package that changed popular culture.

Sadly, my passion for jazz still hasn't caught on with my daughters yet. But I will keep trying. Because jazz was and is America's singular gift to world culture. All popular music follows from jazz.

Either way, the music of our past has become the music of their present. And it's opened new doors for all of us.

We'll go happily talking – or singing – through.

Doody-Doody-Doo, All Over Me

I talked to Mrs. Wizzo!

If you grew up in the Chicago area in the 1960s and 1970s, you'll appreciate what a big deal this is. If you didn't, well, more's the pity for you.

Wizzo the Wacky Wizard, who hailed from Zanzibar, was an integral part of an integral part of the childhood of anyone whose childhood corresponds with those decades – or, as I like to call it, the "Real Bozo Era."

The Real Bozo Era was the 30 or so years in which Bob Bell put on the orange hair and red nose and giant shoes to lead the circus named for his alter-ego, Bozo T. Clown.

People my age watched Bozo and his sidekicks Cookie the Cook (Roy Brown), Oliver O. Oliver (Ray Rayner), Mr. Ned (Ned Locke), Frasier Thomas, and the craziest wizard the world has ever seen, Wizzo (Marshall Brodien) wreak havoc on Bozo's Circus, a.k.a. the WGN television studios, every day over lunch.

Wizzo's nutty magic-inducing spell – he'd chant

"Doody-doody-doo" as he tapped some object with his "Stone of Zanzibar," his sparkling eyes seemingly spinning, making the act look even crazier – often made one wonder what Mr. Brodien might have had to drink before the show.

And then he'd perform a magic trick to outsmart one of this fellow clowns and win a contest to see who could get out of doing some "circus" chore.

It was all hilarious – made even funnier later in early adolescence when it became clear that Bell, Brown, Brodien etc. were often, and obviously, performing as much for themselves and other adults as they were for the children in the studio or television audience.

They'd crack themselves up with double entendres, references to some party, personal habits and inside jokes that no one but them and the other television studio hands got.

But somehow the sheer audacity – remember, they were ostensibly performing for a pre-teen audience in the pre-Britney Spears as Sex Kitten era -- and humor of it came across loud and clear to fans.

My dad was one of the biggest of those fans.

I recently, and quite accidentally, had occasion to talk to Mary Doyle Brodien, a professional writer, and the president of the Tri-Cities branch of the Association of University Women.

I offhandedly asked if she was by chance related to Marshall Brodien.

I was shocked when she said that he is her husband!

Mrs. Wizzo! Alive, real, in the flesh.

Poor woman. I wasted several minutes of her life,

which she will never get back, foolishly gushing about the great joy that Wizzo brought to my life.

Telling her dumb stories about how my dad for years and years – well after I stopped watching the show, Bob Bell retired and that other guy (an imposter if ever there was one) took over the giant red shoes – would conjure up Wizzo's incantation: "Doody-doody-doo!"

My dad would perform this craziness shamelessly. His act certainly would have landed him in a nuthouse if we didn't already know that he was crazier than anyone there, even for our friends and girlfriends, whether they understood the reference or not.

He even once made his own "Stone of Zanzibar" to fully carry the effect. That's just the kind of fun-loving clown that my dad was.

I don't know about my brothers. But I was never embarrassed as teens often are, of my dad when he did these things. And trust me, his Wizzo impersonations were just one of his many bits of schtick.

The man was a natural born entertainer. Bozo's circus was one of our few real connections.

Strange as it may sound, I didn't have a whole lot in common with my dad, an old-school cop and hard-core conservative who openly and absolutely loathed the media.

I have written before that my dad taught me only three essential things: Sean Connery is the only real James Bond; John Wayne is the greatest American actor ever; and that you never, even if hell is freezing over, bet against the Chicago Bears.

But my conversation with Mrs. Brodien reminded

me of this other point of connection. Silly, yes. Odd, perhaps.

But it is a connection as precious and joy-filled as watching "Goldfinger" for the hundredth time; seeing the Duke beat the hell out of Bruce Dern, playing one of Hollywood's nastiest bad-guys ever in "The Cowboys"; or celebrating another Bears victory over the Packers.

May every dad share something with their kids as magical as Wizzo the World's Wackiest Wizard.

Doody-doody-doo, indeed.

Moving Out, Moving Up, Moving On

Of course, it had to happen.

For many, it is the whole reason they buy a house in the first place -- to sell it.

So, admittedly it was inevitable, the springing up of "For Sale" signs in a neighborhood, like bugs slowly multiplying on the scrumptious petals and leaves of a rose.

Recently, numerous houses around our home have gone on the block. The timing is about right. Most of the houses were built between three and five years ago, mainly sold to young families looking for their first digs.

The building in this part of our subdivision is over. So the market, a little less saturated with houses that look just like those for sale, is again ready to pass along a bit of a profit.

Families that five years ago comprised two adults and a baby or two, now boast two adults, several young kids, maybe a pet or two, and several years of accumulated stuff. Ears carefully attuned can almost hear the houses groaning under the extra burden.

Yet it is a hard thing to confront, this neighborhood change, because people occupy those houses.

And those people have shared experiences and dreams and hardships and triumphs. They have celebrated births and birthdays. Commiserated about utility bills. Groused about slow snow plowing.

Tended to each other's kids' boo-boos or crowed when they learned to ride without training wheels. Shared a private smile when their kids at the unknowing, innocent age of five solemnly declared they are "boyfriend" and "girlfriend."

They have learned to exist and coexist in a different world – a world created for them by some long-gone, invisible developer, but shaped by them, together.

It hasn't always been peachy, what with the kids' skirmishes and the adults' infrequent short-lived (but at the time, very real) anger with each other over one thing or another.

Yet, they have managed to turn the initial caution in the question, "Who are those people?" into relationships built on the trust and need inherent in queries like "Can you watch the kids tonight?" And sometimes, in the best cases, mutual faith, respect and love leads to very big requests like "Would you be godparents to my child?"

They have become friends. They have become family.

So, what does one do when a family member decides to leave?

One could be jealous, selfishly wondering, "How

in the world can they afford to move anyway, when we can't?"

Or angry, your heart secretly singed by that creeping feeling of desertion – the feeling that they're leaving just when their friendship, private camaraderie, sense of humor or sunshine smile are most needed.

Or just plain sad for the loss of people whom have come to be important parts of your daily life.

But perhaps the best thing is to not "be" anything, but rather to just Be.

My pastor recently delivered a wonderful, thoughtful sermon about how we use time. "Chronos" time, he said, addresses what we do in time. Our modern lives – defined and directed by clocks and calendars, planners and palm pilots – are all about "chronos" time.

But, our lives need to be much more about "kairos" time. Time spent just "being," rather than "doing." Kairos time is about building connections and being in relationship with each other.

Kids are the best at living in kairos time. Like the children who often draw adults together in the first place, we need to just live directly in and for the moment. Spend time with our closest friends, especially as they prepare for what is surely a monumental step for them.

Moving, even under the best circumstances, is never easy.

Share the joy-filled excitement inherent in the adventure facing the soon-to-be relocated. Know that a family separated is still a family. Real friends don't disappear just because they live in a different ZIP code.

That's the wonderful thing about true community. "For Sale" signs may signal a changing of the neighborhood, but not its death. True community is built -- and depends and thrives -- on the kind of spirit that distance can't erase.

Enjoy the relationships you have now, instead of dwelling on what might be lost. Or even contemplating what might come next. Because, just as someone had to sell their house, someone else will buy it.

And you'll again wonder, "Who are those people?"

The Toughest Job Ever? Just Ask Mom

A blind brain surgeon. The guy who numbers each dollar bill. An elephant stall cleaner.

With Mother's Day coming Sunday, I was trying to think recently of jobs that were harder than motherhood.

There aren't many, considering everything that moms deal with and are responsible for daily. Even under the easiest conditions, (and honestly, is giving birth ever easy?) motherhood is perhaps the most involving, heartening, frustrating, challenging and rewarding endeavor humans face.

I'm comfortably in touch with my feminine side. But, knowing what she went through raising three boys, I can honestly say I wouldn't want to be my mom.

My mother married young and birthed my middle brother and myself within three years. But it didn't take long to realize her marriage was going nowhere fast.

A divorce was followed by a second marriage to the man whose name I share by adoption. The second marriage was better, but not great. It largely reflected my dad's life interests: he loved being a cop and father, and liked being a husband.

My youngest brother was born a few years later, giving my mother three sons and a husband – himself a fourth son, by any fair reckoning -- by her mid-20s.

The person on the receiving end of a knife throwing act. The guy shot out of a circus cannon. The KISS concert cleanup crew.

Like most moms, mine can and does drive me nuts many days. Even now – especially now -- that we're married she tries to choreograph my brothers' and my lives.

She's certainly not perfect. But then, neither were we.

Through our youth, we gave my mom as much as many people could handle. We each dated regularly, and took part in many school and extracurricular activities that neither parent was immediately familiar with.

For example, my mom wasn't always a sports fan. But she became a football expert, and even learned to love the Chicago Bears, my dad's favorite team.

She suffered the indignity of the Abe Gibron-Neal Armstrong-Dave Wannstedt eras – not to mention supporting and sitting through scores of youth league and high school football games, band performances, tennis matches and paintball tournaments for the sake of husband and sons.

When many other women sought jobs and their "identities" outside the home, my mom held the traditional, and certainly less-glamorous front.

She served as taxi service; maid; laundry woman;

cook; teacher; counselor; law enforcement; domestic engineer; negotiator; mediator; and referee of dozens of fall acorn fights between my brothers, father and me.

And those were the good days. Both of my brothers liberally tested the parentally-set borders around their teen years. (I did too, though to a lesser extent.)

Like many cops, my dad's temper ran in only two gears – fast, and faster. So Mom's dual challenge was to mete out sufficient discipline to keep us from becoming gutter trash, while also protecting us from my dad's potentially more severe response to our youthful indiscretions.

Setting aside all the usual child-parent differences of opinion, I'd say that she did pretty well.

Three boys of varying temperaments, interests and inclinations are each unjailed, gainfully employed and married, two raising kids of our own. And none of us has yet needed psychiatric attention for dressing up in her clothes while living in a roadside motel.

Jackhammer operator. Battery supplier to the Energizer Bunny. Old West gunslinger.

Widowed too young at 51, she is relearning the dance of the single. But even as my mom tries to figure out the parameters of her new life, she still tries to make mine easier.

Need a babysitter? Call Grandma. Need a vehicle while ours is in the shop? Mom will let us use hers. Need a temporary loan? No problem. And she, unlike those scurrilous banks, never sets repayment deadlines or charges interest.

Cop. Firefighter. Lawyer. Doctor. Teacher. The presidency.

No, I can't think of a more demanding or important job than being a mother. And Hallmark's vast card collection can't properly thank my mom, and all moms for what she's given, and continues to give. So this Mother's Day, over a nice brunch I'll just say I love you, Mom.

Uh, by the way: Can you front me a few bucks for the lunch tab? I'll pay you back, I promise.

Thank the Bum for America

The man – some might describe him as a vagrant, a bum – sat on the steps of the United States capitol building.

Even from a distance it was clear that he was dirty, his clothes tattered. He held a cardboard sign with the words, "I am a Vietnam veteran. My country has abandoned me. Please help."

He did nothing else. Just sat there with his sign. And yet, nearly 18 years later, this experience remains one of the most powerful I have ever had.

Simply, it embodies the truest vision of American life and American freedom.

American life, because these kinds of scenes – the poorest of our poor literally and publicly begging for help -- play so routinely that that have become background to our daily lives. We acknowledge them, if at all, only as a passing curiosity or, if they dare to violate our personal space, as an irritation.

And American freedom, because in nearly any other country, such a person would disappear. Probably thrown into a dark jail cell or just shot. Never to be seen or heard from again.

Only in America can a person openly take his government to task – sitting on the steps of the government itself, no less – and live to tell about it. What a fascinating and sad and great symbol of what makes our country special.

This column is a Memorial Day tribute to all of the men and women of our armed services who have fallen to protect and uphold the rights of a nation free to criticize itself.

A nation free to laugh at – and hopefully learn from -- its many contradictions and flaws.

A nation free to point out the idiocies of its leaders and hope and wish and work for a better crop the next time around.

A nation free, thanks to their dedication and sacrifice.

And it seems wrong, even insulting to those in the armed services – not to mention the police, fire and other public safety agencies – to trot out these thoughts only once or twice a year.

We should honor and respect and thank the military for its duty and service every day. It is not enough to watch the occasional war movie, shed a tear and head out to the backyard to barbecue another burger.

We may not agree with the methods of ensuring our freedom. As we've seen in Iraq, such a goal often demands tactics that might not sit well with the "average American."

But the burden of this battle often demands methods equal to the sacrifice. The idea of pain and death is never pleasant, whether it's being suffered by our foes or by our soldiers.

Still, what they are asked to do, and indeed what they often do, is so far beyond the range of understanding of the "average American" that it cannot be thought of like anything else.

Quite simply, our armed forces are asked to kill others and die themselves so that we don't have to. And why? To protect an idea – freedom -- something both so nebulous and real that it is worth killing and dying for.

That's why soldiers of today are in some ways more impressive than those of an older vintage, who were forced into service by the government. These young people in the military today – and they are almost always very young – volunteer for their service.

Now, they may do so with the idea that they're going to learn job skills or gain an education that will punch their ticket later in life. But ultimately, always, they know that they are called to kill and be killed. For the older generations of soldiers, the military was a requirement. Today, it is a choice. A hard, mean, terrible, but necessary choice.

Which brings me back to the story of the veteran on the Capitol steps.

We ask and require and equip our soldiers to commit what in real life would be heinous crimes to protect us.

We put them in the direct, oncoming path of death itself.

And then we (in the form of our government) do not do enough to care for those lucky enough to do that terrible chore and come out alive.

Right up there with slavery, the white Europeans'

genocide of the Native Americans and the internment of Japanese-Americans during WWII, this is a travesty of which we should all be ashamed.

That soldier sitting on the steps of the capitol was right. His government did abandon him.

And in a strange, vexing twist of fate and design, the very fact that he was able to say so, makes America the greatest country in the world.

We're not always right, or righteous. But whatever we are, it is due to people like him.

The Gospel According to John

I was talking to John Mellencamp the other day…

Ok, well, not actually talking to him. Actually he was more talking to me…

Ok, well, not actually talking to me. Actually he was more talking about me – or at least about my life -- through several songs on his magnificent new CD, "Life, Death, Love and Freedom."

Mellencamp and I have had these kinds of conversations for more than two decades. I heard personal messages in his Midwestern rock back when he was still (unfortunately and amusingly) named Cougar.

Then, the songs were about young life, young love, rebellion, and the power of rock-and-roll. The world of the 20-something from Indiana making music for a world of fans that looked and lived and thought like him.

As he aged, I aged. As he learned about the harder edges of real life, I learned about the harder edges of real life. As he thought bigger thoughts, I thought bigger thoughts. As he got wiser and sharper…well, I thought bigger thoughts.

Anyway, here we both are now in middle age (me early, him more middle/late). His latest collection finds us both peeking at life's rearview mirror, wondering where the time went, what the future holds, and if what we have done with our lives amounts to much at all in the big picture.

The opening lines from the song "Don't Need This Body" sum up my mental, not to mention my physical state in recent months:

"This getting older/Ain't for cowards/This getting older/Is a lot to go through/Ain't gonna need this body/Much longer/Ain't gonna need this body/Much more"

Exactly.

Then "Longest Days" hit me like a ball-peen hammer between the eyes: "It seems like once upon a time ago/I was where I was supposed to be/My vision was true and my heart was too/There was no end to what I could dream/I walked like a hero into the setting sun/Everyone called out my name/Death to me was just a mystery/I was too busy raisin' up Cain/

"But nothing lasts forever/Your best efforts don't always pay/Sometimes you get sick/And you don't get better/That's when life is short/Even in its longest days."

Spoken like a man who has seen his world from the top of the top, and now finds himself somewhere around the middle wondering how and when he got there.

And I am telling you, Mellencamp may not have been literally talking to me, but I heard him loud and clear as sure as if he was sharing a cup of coffee across my kitchen table.

Strictly, a poem of mine called "Just" ponders some of these same thoughts:

The weight of mediocrity
is a foot across my throat

The odor of arrogance soured, spilled
on youth steals my breath away

A memory lifted by laughter
of time spent on the roof
believing, knowing that I could fly
Maybe not today, but definitely

Remembering a boast, floating on
wings lifted by jet-streaming confidence
Five years would make me Royko
and 10, Ernest's ghost in new khakis

Tomorrow became today became yesterday
and no wings, no Parisian "Feast"
Sliced bread is still the greatest thing
God's gift going elsewhere, always

Now I laugh to cool the fire of tears
Drawn to the harsh light of my reality
crashing against dead dreams, knowing
that I am just…just…just…

That was written more than 10 years ago…before my knees ached with every step.

Before my gut threatened bodily harm if I dared to try to lose weight.

Before my eyes began fighting their own personal

battle between near-sightedness and far-sightedness, mocking my vain decision to ignore my wife's urging to get bifocals.

Back when "the boys next door" were just rhetorical fodder for entertaining conversation about my daughters, not actual monosyllabic shadows lurking in my garage each summer night.

Before I hit, you know, "middle age."

All of which raises an interesting, infuriating question: how does one measure progress at the midpoint of existence, as one slides inexorably down the other side of the hill of life?

Jeez, that last paragraph reads like such a downer. Sorry about that. But I mean it more as an honest inquiry. Just as parenting doesn't come with a manual, there are no clear directions about living.

Have goals and dreams, sure. Aspire to be the very best at whatever one does, absolutely. Faith in a higher power certainly lights life's path. A good family and friends provide support and love. A good job, if one is so blessed, helps to acquire the material things both necessary for daily living and wanted for entertainment and pleasure.

But what does it mean when one doesn't make all of ones goals? Or never rises to the top of his or her chosen field? Or finds faith lacking? Or has a lousy family? Or never seems to make enough money? Does that constitute failure? Or am I taking it all too seriously?

I guess I'll have to wait until I die – or for my good friend John's next CD – to learn the answer. Hopefully, the new CD will arrive first.

Big Questions from Little Mouths

Children are only as dumb as adults let them be.

I suppose that sounds obvious, but the thought struck me as a great insight.

My youngest daughter Olivia, who is 7 (or seven-and-a-half, as she has reminded us since the day she turned seven,) recently asked my wife if the sky fell, would God fall down with it?

Now on one level the query certainly strikes a child-ish chord. But really, that's a big, big question.

On the occasion of our children's return to school this week it also seemed an opportune time to explore the importance of education and learning.

My youngest progeny's thought was so big, in fact, that it would send many adults scurrying in the other direction.

I know plenty of people over the age of seven, some in the professional ministerial ranks, who wouldn't even begin to think such thoughts. Their thousands-year-old dogma has built a wall too tall for their small theology -- and insight, not to mention faith -- to scale.

Too high, too scary. Thoughts, ideas, notions, suggestions that go against the grain -- no matter what way the grain goes or how it got there -- often strike adults that way.

But children, they're a different breed altogether.

They think. They ask. They wonder. There are no walls around their curiosity, no borders on their brilliance. Except those that we adults put there.

I don't believe that any well-meaning parent puts such constraints on their children maliciously.

Of course, I have been told that my Christian optimism often leaves both of my feet planted firmly on naiveté when it comes to people's good intentions. But let's just agree for the sake of argument that most parents sincerely intend to encourage their kids' intelligence most of the time.

So what happens on the trip between the two major "hoods" in all of our lives -- child and adult?

In some cases, adults just don't know the answer. But instead of taking the time to find it out with their inquisitive child, they blow it off. A simple "I don't know" suffices when a trip to the Internet, library or (dinosaur of dinosaurs) the encyclopedia is in order.

Such behavior is damnable. After all, if you give a child a fish, and she'll eat. Teach a child to fish, and she'll learn how to feed herself.

Likewise, say, "I don't know" when she asks what's for dinner, and you've created someone who will waste a lifetime buying take-out and never know the joys of cooking.

In other cases, the adult is worried about the ramifications of the answer.

This is especially the case with especially big questions like "the meaning of life."

Where do babies come from?

If there is a God, how did September 11 (and myriad other evil things) happen?

Is there a Santa Claus?

Where is the line drawn between jazz, blues and R&B?

Is it better to do the right thing for the wrong reason, or the wrong thing for the right reason?

Why do ladybugs have spots?

How does democracy work when, by all rights, it should collapse on itself?

How do flies fly since they're engineered all wrong?

Will the Cubs ever, ever, ever win the World Series?

Ok, perhaps the last one is too big for mere mortals. But you get the point…

I make no claims for genius. Trust me, it's a daily struggle to keep up with the world around me, much less to gain any significant ground on the world's "Deep Thoughts."

Likewise I am certain I won't win any innovative parenting awards. But that's the beauty of this whole idea.

Encouraging our children to learn; supporting their natural inquisitiveness; fueling their enthusiasm; pointing them toward (and to the degree possible, providing) good resources; and teaching them that learning is a lifelong, valuable, enjoyable, meaningful endeavor, doesn't cost much of anything at all.

The only real price is time, and patience, and love. Perhaps a good book shared together, or a few hours lying in the grass studying earthworms together.

But the benefits will fill a world of libraries.

<u>Words: The Toothpaste of Everyday Life</u>

"If."

That's the answer to the riddle, "What is the biggest word in the English language?"

The two-letter word throws open a thousand doors, conveys of a thousand dreams and carries the burden of a thousand regrets. As in, "What if I had done this, rather than that?"

It should go without saying, but language is a very powerful thing. (That's something of a joke there – saying that it goes without saying that language…well, anyway, I thought it was clever…)

One word, can change everything, positively or negatively. Philosophically and materially.

The notion that we should measure our words carefully, whether written or spoken, occurs to me often – usually after saying something that would have been better kept to myself. That what we say, and how we say it, is essential to our relationships, society, history and the human condition.

Every idea, every word, every jot and tittle used to express ourselves means something.

For example, I recently attended a worship service which included the Apostle's Creed: "We believe in God, the Father almighty, creator of heaven and earth," etc.

Years ago I read a fascinating, challenging and thought provoking bit of biblical scholarship about the Creed.

In an early version of the Creed, the scholar suggested, there was a "period" after the word "suffered" in the phrase, "Jesus…suffered under Pontius Pilate, was crucified, died, and was buried."

If true, the single punctuation mark, perhaps the slimmest, slightest, smallest, of linguistic markers, radically alters the meaning, tone and message of the Creed. Try it both ways.

In its current Canonical form, the Creed suggests that Jesus suffered under Pontius Pilate – only. The rest of his life, it seems, was, relatively speaking, a bowl of cherries – or more historically accurate, a bowl of figs.

Now, read it again, but stop after "suffered". Jesus suffered. Throughout his life, regularly, even daily. This one slight change paints an entirely different picture of the life Jesus led, of His human experience.

But enough of biblical scholarship.

This bit of critical supposition reminds me to communicate as clearly, concisely and precisely as possible.

Our language is as feeble, weak and flawed as we are. And so we must use it carefully.

Say what you mean, mean what you say.

Be careful what you ask for. You might get it.

Words are like toothpaste. Once they're out, it's awfully hard to put them back in.

These are all vital, life lessons. They have little to do with age, and everything to do with maturity.

As parents, we've tried to impart this wisdom to our girls as they fight with each other, saying hurtful things in the heat of sibling rivalry. It's good to apologize later, but better to first think about what might come out of your mouth, and perhaps put a cork in it before damage is done.

The mature person knows when to speak. And, more importantly, when not to. Miles Davis and Ernest Hemingway, both renowned for their ability to communicate ideas, were famous for what they didn't say.

Hemingway mastered and promoted spare prose. Davis' music was celebrated as much for the space between the notes as for the notes he played.

The wise person knows the value and power of his words, and so uses them judiciously. Not wanting to hurt or unnecessarily offend, he is thoughtful about what he says, and when, and to whom.

None of which is to say I'm any kind of expert or model for this kind of communication.

I spend hours crafting these columns and other things I write. Pouring over each word, thesaurus and dictionary and reference books at hand. Turning the exact phrase. Measuring meter and sentence length. Listening to the flow of each paragraph.

And then my wife or kids will say some innocent thing which, for no good reason, strikes me the wrong way. Then, something stupid flies out of my mouth like raw sewage out of a pipe.

Hurtful. Dumb. Mean. Thoughtless. Pointless.

Apologies are made, and usually accepted. Thank God, I am blessed with an understanding and forgiving family.

But my challenge – our challenge, as human beings – is to pick what we say with the same care with which we pick out our clothes or any of the millions of lesser important things that dominate our lives.

Our words speak to who we are, deep down. They are the bridges between us. They are the foundations on which we build our relationships. We should be honest, yes, and candid, certainly.

And we should also be respectful and caring and thoughtful in what we say. Our ability to speak and write lifts us – barely – above animals.

Communicating carelessly, thoughtlessly abdicating the gift of language, puts us right back in the muck.

Sleeping the Good Sleep of Justice

His face a pretzel of anger and disgust, the young juror finally agreed to acquit the defendant. But before signing his name to the verdict, he stated his real feelings in no uncertain terms. "This is wrong. I won't sleep tonight. The law sucks."

I could understand his emotion and his position. But the young man was flat-wrong.

I recently served a week of jury duty. I shared my fellow juror's outrage when we eventually voted to send home a Chicago man who, the prosecutors had told us, had been told had been twice convicted before of the same charge of possessing and intending to deliver heroin.

The justice system is strange.

It forces innocent people into intimate contact with the dangerous, the vile, the unsympathetic in our society. It magnifies every flaw in the defendant's character. Every bad decision. Every life mistake. Every bias, hatred and violent tendency.

It reminds those who generally respect the law that

there are others who just as generally "flip the bird" to the law with one hand, while clutching and waving with the other riches that crime often awards to those stupid enough to pursue it.

And after all that, the justice system does the worst thing of all. It reminds us that we are all the same.

The law abiders and the lifelong criminals. We all are born the same. We all die the same. And throughout our lives, virtuous or filled with vice, we get the same protections under the law.

A slap in the face? Maybe immediately.

But long term, the sting of that slap is softened by the comfort of knowing that our system tries its best to ignore everything but the facts– which are just as often down and dirty as they are high and righteous -- in the struggle for real justice.

The 12 of us knew in our collective gut that the defendant, Johnny, would likely resume trafficking drugs. Probably as fast as he could get to a cell phone after the trial ended.

No matter. True enough, a Department of Corrections officer searching all cars entering Stateville prison last summer found a foil packet tucked into the inside brim of Johnny's baseball cap. And inside that foil was less than a tenth of a gram of heroin.

Possession, clearly. And on penal grounds, without doubt. Two felonies, two charges.

But no conviction.

See, Johnny claimed that the hat and the drugs belonged to his brother, also a Chicago drug dealer several-times-convicted.

Sure, he'd been in trouble for this very thing before,

Johnny testified. But this time, he had simply put on a hat picked up in the house he shares with his brother. His brother testified – looking stoned even as he slouched in the witness chair – that the hat and drugs were indeed his.

The argument from two convicted felons wearing more gold jewelry than the entire jury combined, who gambled at Harrah's casino over lunch the day deliberations started was arrogant and stupid. It flew in the face of logic. It thumbed its nose at common sense. But it was enough for the law.

The law requires the jury to be certain that the defendant knew that he had the drugs when he left the house. It was written that way for a reason. Perhaps so that people won't be punished for innocent mistakes like driving a friend's car unaware that there's a loaded gun under the seat – or even, wearing a relative's hat not knowing that there's heroin in the brim.

Whatever really happened, the police presented no evidence to connect Johnny with the drugs before he was searched at Stateville (the cops even gave the hat back!) and the prosecutor did a poor job presenting admittedly weak evidence.

The evidence didn't support the charge, and so an obviously guilty man walked free. The only consolation was the hope that the system will do a better job next time.

I am the son of a cop. And my heart told me things about Johnny that I believed were true. This was not a good guy. He had done wrong before, and very likely would again.

But my head kept going back to the single word: knowingly possess. Did he knowingly possess?

I hated signing those acquittal forms, too. But I couldn't say Johnny knew. So the law worked. For Johnny. For us.

And I slept fine.

Not Closing the Door

Would you do the same?

Imagine that you're home from work for a quick lunch.

The doorbell rings. You open it. Standing there is a man you've never seen before.

Kindly enough, the man – of a different race – says he can tell that you, a single woman approaching middle age, need your gutters cleaned.

He adds that he's been waiting for you to come home. Waiting for a moment to talk to you. To offer his services.

You try to ignore the tingling sense of foreboding -- the flare of fear, a warning knotting your gut.

The hype, created and fueled by years of media screaming, rings like a bell, reminding you that everyone who looks, thinks, acts, talks, dresses differently is – must be – a creep, a menace, a danger. Cannot be trusted. Should be feared, suspected, avoided.

But you don't close the door with a polite but firm

"Thanks, but no thanks" as so many – indeed, most – would have done by now.

The man goes on.

He'll clean the gutters, the man offers. But he'll have to charge you double his normal rate because he can tell that the gutters haven't been cleaned in years and the debris is really compacted.

See, he's had a really bad run of luck. His house was damaged by the recent tornado. He lost his job. And his kids will soon go back to school. He needs money for school supplies, the man says.

He and his family intend to start a landscaping business, but he needs the boost right now just to get over the hump.

In the time it takes to listen to his story, your mind, like a cynical supercomputer, rifles through all of the obvious options:

He's a con-man. He's casing your house. He's looking for an easy hand-out. He's picked you as an easy mark. You'll give him money and he'll never return…

Or, the option least obvious, least likely, at least in the eyes and minds and hearts of this untrusting, unfaithful, unwelcoming world:

That the man is telling the truth.

Standing there, your lunch waiting, your gutters full, your mind racing, your stomach flip-flopping from nerves as much as hunger, you make a brave, bold and brash decision:

"Yes, you can clean my gutters," you tell the man.

This act of radical faith is soon tested when the man calls back a few days later. Yes, he's due to come back and finish up a job. But his van broke down. Will you come pick up him, his wife and four kids so that he can do the work he promised to do?

And when you do, he asks one more thing: will you float him $10 to go buy a fast food breakfast?

Each request is another test of your trust. Another opportunity to be left just a little bit poorer if he chooses to call you "Sucker" and run.

But he doesn't run. And you continue to show a faith, a courage, a humility, a belief in inherent honesty and human goodness that is so rare these days that it borders on the irrational, the unreasonable, the remarkable.

And how is your hospitality repaid?

Just as he promised.

Clean gutters. Fifteen bags of yard waste collected and removed that you would have never gotten to, not even if you wanted to – and you never wanted to.

Meanwhile, the man continues to make an honest wage. With your help he earns by the sweat of his brow another day's reprieve from the storms life often blows into the lives of the poor.

Who knows? You may still be ripped off.

But even if it happens, even if your faith and kindness is stolen along with that last advance payment for work that may never get done, you can know that you have done the right thing for the right reasons.

Someone needed help, and you helped.

This is a true story.

It happened to a close relative. A woman who, for nearly 20 years, I have respected and come to love for her independence and generosity. Now, my admiration has increased exponentially for her courage.

It's a great reminder that hospitality is required of us

as human beings. Not because it will earn us anything. But because it is the right thing to do.

The person who came knocking could be anyone – a neighbor, a relative, you. It doesn't really matter. The bottom line is the same.

Most of the time our dreams work out just as planned. Sometimes though, reality snags the edges of our dreams, turning them into popped party balloons sadly littering the floor of life.

Sometimes, when their dreams die, dreamers need a little help. A little faith, a little trust.

It is sad that some would, and do, take advantage of kindness like that which this woman showed.

But it is sadder still that so many of us would have just closed the door.

A Handful of Change

The woman approached, clad in a fur coat.

And if the fur hadn't actually clothed a critter at one point, the diamond on her hand was big enough to make any reasonable person think she was wealthy enough to at least invest in a mink farm.

She neared, and I rang the Salvation Army bell with everything I had. Partly out of enthusiasm for the opportunity to help people who needed it. And partly to fend off the biting cold.

Yet, despite my best efforts to earn a few coins, perhaps a dollar or two, she blew by, eyes averted, colder than the bitter winter wind that froze my smile in place.

For several years in the middle 1990s I had the pleasure of ringing a bell for the Salvation Army in the Northwest suburbs, where I worked.

This scene played consistently – sadly, frustratingly – at least once, and in some cases several times, every time I took the station in front of a store.

People who looked like they could most afford to give a lot, often gave very little.

Conversely, those who appeared the most destitute, the most in need themselves – the ones for whom we were supposedly ringing those bells -- often dug most deeply to drop a handful of coins into that red bucket.

This memory returned recently for several reasons. Most especially, because we're entering the time of year when we celebrate family, love, joy, success – those things in our lives which bind us together.

Yet, for many, the holiday season is fraught with heartache, loneliness, separation, failure – the realities of lives ripped apart.

The memory also came back because of the current economic state in our country and community.

As major companies continue to lay people off, as the American automobile industry drives on like a car with three flat tires, as the financial market limps along, afraid to lend anything among itself much less to "little people" like us, lots of people are losing jobs. Losing life savings. Losing houses.

Losing hope.

And of course, the memory of my bell ringing experience returned because of the immensely important events that occurred last week. Not that an African American was elected president of this great country. That was inevitable (though still wonderful.)

But that a thinking and thoughtful person was elected. Someone capable of seeing and understanding and caring about the bigger picture.

Someone whose emotional maturity is light years beyond the temporary and visceral joy of bombing first and asking questions later. Someone more interested in engaging and challenging our intellect rather than forging and playing off of our fear.

Someone who will bring true change. Not change merely in the names of the players. But change that matters. Change in the way we see ourselves and see others.

Someone who embodies and imbues hope.

Put all of those thoughts together, and those dark memories rushed back, dragging along impressions of human nature's natural cynicism.

When it comes to my fellow homo sapiens my goofy mind often runs to the dark. If not typical, then at least understandable for the son of a cop and reporter.

There is a lot of sadness in this world, much of it self-inflicted.

Cultural ignorance, emotional immaturity, selfishness, jealousy, mistrust – and the politics that support these destructive and pointless responses to the world around us -- have created an "I, me, mine" American society.

These elements of our humanity are at the bleached-blond roots of the snooty dismissal that woman gave me that wintry day years ago. I could see it in her demeanor as she blew by me: "Why should I help *those* people?" "Those" could be any variation of the word "different".

But it doesn't have to be this way. It shouldn't be this way.

We can change ourselves. And through our own change, we can change others. We can change our community and the world around us. Change is often difficult. Yet, as the saying goes, most things worth doing, are hard.

This holiday season find ways to help others.

Give to your favorite charity. Give to your place of worship. Donate to your local food pantry or second hand clothing store. Pull a tag from one of those "holiday trees" and buy a gift for a stranger.

And, the next time you hear that ringing bell, throw some money into that red bucket. Better yet, have your kids do it. Teach them the lesson of God and grace and giving early on. They, and you, will be the better for it.

This is not about politics. But by all social/cultural/political definitions, Jesus was a liberal. He gave His life to change the world.

Thankfully, no one is asking for that. A handful of change will do just fine.

Related By Love

I am a half-breed, once removed. And I couldn't be happier about it.

This is the kind of concept that can boggle some people's minds into oatmeal – the ones who try to figure out that "2nd cousin on my mother's side, twice removed by marriage" kind of stuff.

But actually, this couldn't be easier.

My mom divorced my biological father and re-married when I was about two years old. My dad – the one who raised me and shaped my life, not the one who sired me to give me life – legally adopted me and my then-infant brother. He considered us his sons. And, like most fathers, he wanted his children to have his most prized possession – his name.

Few things have had more of an impact in my life, both positive and negative, than my surname.

There has been the amused confusion of people staring at me, trying to connect the dots between my Mexican last name and my clearly-not-Mexican complexion and features.

There has been the overt racism of people assuming that I should speak Spanish just because of my last name, and holding it against me when they learn that I don't.

And the subtle racism of those who make ethnic jokes and derogatory comments about Mexicans in my presence, never thinking (or caring?) that while I may not be Mexican by blood, I count myself as half-Mexican by association.

There has been the weird, dual sense of being both an insider and an outsider in ways both obvious and hidden. It's a small boat that has carried me down life's stream. Not many people can claim to have pulled the same oars as I have. Sometimes the unique double-layered nature of my name has put me in a good place. Other times it's left me out in the cold.

Then of course there is the mind-twisting fascination of watching my wife, who is whiter even than I, and my daughters – particularly my youngest, who is a Scandinavian doll, as fair-skinned as her mother – also live life with a Latino tag.

It is one thing for me to have done so all my life. I at least had my father to point to, either metaphorically or literally. But since he died 10 years ago, his daughter-in-law and granddaughters (whom he barely had time to get to know) don't enjoy that same privilege.

And there is the love of great food and music, the (brief, now-gone) dual language skills, and most of all, the awareness of and appreciation for people of all walks of life that came from growing up with my dad's family.

I share this because I will spend part of this Christmas

weekend with the people whom I call family, though we look nothing alike, share no blood, do not enjoy a common tongue and have not seen each other for several years.

What we do share, however, is love.

The greatest, most common and yet most challenging bond of all.

Love does not know or care that my father was my father (officially, technically) only on paper.

It just knows and cares that he chose me, raised me, supported me, encouraged me, saw me over many life hurdles and not once let anyone know that he had not been in the hospital delivery room at the exact moment I left my mother's womb.

Indeed, my dad made up so many (often-hilarious) stories about his supposed involvement in our birth, and his telling of them was so convincing, that no one would have ever doubted the veracity of his tales, no matter how tall.

He was far, far from perfect. A man with a bad temper and a 1950s mentality perfectly suited to the old-school cop that he was my dad had his share of faults and then some.

Still, in a world full of selfish people doing selfish things for their own selfish gain, he gave. A lot. And his – my – family continues to represent my dad to me now.

My life, good, bad and ugly, is directly linked to a man who fell in love with a young waitress and took on the challenge/burden/benefit of her children as his own.

How successful he was depends on how you define success. That's a life lesson gleaned from my father, who could see the good in many people callously and shallowly disregarded. Perspective in all things means a lot.

Perhaps the best gift my dad left though was a simple, realistic appreciation for life. Not every day is good. But more days than not are better than what the world, and sometimes our own hearts and minds, would have us believe.

Seek and see the good. Honor family and friends. Celebrate life's gifts. Whatever they look like, however they come.

Chaplin, Ali, James Brown: Greatness Changing the World

Lately, I've been pondering "greatness."

Not my own. Heaven forbid. What I do falls so short of greatness that pondering it wouldn't take very long at all. It would barely approach "pon". And then only if you, dear reader, out of the kind generosity of your heart, were to spot me the "p" and the "o".

No, my thinking has been more about the nature of greatness. What makes something or someone great? What impact does greatness have? Why does it matter? Why do we care if something is great?

This notion noodled across my cranium a few weekends ago while watching Charlie Chaplin's first talkie, "The Great Dictator," his masterpiece about a Jewish barber who looks like a European dictator (who looks like Adolph Hitler).

Like a chef creating a kitchen masterpiece so complicated that no one else could do it – but making it look so easy that everyone felt like they could – Chaplin crafted cinematic magic.

His movies, especially those he single-handedly wrote, produced, directed and scored (yes, he wrote most of the music for his films, too) were light years beyond anything that anyone else was doing.

They combined smart satire and social commentary (increasingly sharp as he got older, becoming vitriolic, sometimes dark and even bitter) with physical comedy so beautifully, painstakingly choreographed that Fred Astaire had to be secretly, nervously taking notes.

Through his movies, Chaplin changed the world. He was, simply, great.

Then, the news broke that Russian author Aleksandr Solzhenitsyn died.

Solzhenitsyn helped to bring down the Soviet Union through his masterpieces exposing the country's repressive inner workings during the Stalin era.

"One Day in the Life of Ivan Denisovitch" and "The Gulag Archipelago" both painted dark portraits of life inside Soviet prison/work camps where Solzhenitsyn himself lived and labored for eight years, because he dared to write a letter criticizing Stalin. The stories are all the more terrifying because they are true.

His fingerprints were on the bricks from the fallen Berlin Wall, as surely as those of George Bush (the First), Pope John Paul (the Second) or Ronald Reagan (the Only).

His courageous work to shine a light on a shadowy system few could even imagine, much less believe existed – a system at which he openly and publicly thumbed his nose as if to say "I am not afraid of you" – changed the world. Solzhenitsyn was, simply, great.

The Gods of Greatness must have been reading my

mind, because shortly after, an article appeared about a new DVD collection including James Brown's famous concert in Boston on April 5, 1968 – the day after Dr. Martin Luther King Jr.'s assassination.

After briefly considering canceling the show, Brown opted to perform at the mayor's request to honor King's memory.

Brown used his masterful, spellbinding performance to reassure and remind the audience about Dr. King's messages of peace. He kept a crowd of 15,000 angry, hurting young black Americans from rioting as other major American cities exploded.

Brown changed popular music. Given white musicians' penchant for ripping off black music, it is fair to say that there wouldn't be any popular music after James Brown, if there hadn't been a James Brown.

But more importantly, Brown, a politically astute, savvy businessman, a commanding presence in the black community and beyond, became perhaps the most powerful figure in black America during the 1960s and early 1970s. When James Brown said it, "it" became "IT".

James Brown changed the world. He was, simply, great.

There are, of course, many more examples.

But these three, and others one might offer by thumbing through the daily news, beg the question – is greatness simply creating an impact? Causing a reaction? Forcing a shift? Changing the way something is done or understood?

Yes. And no.

Certainly all of those factors factor in. But, for

example, Olympic swimmer Michael Phelps has won eight gold medals (so far). He's a damned good swimmer. Perhaps the best ever. But is he "great"? Not hardly.

Muhammad Ali though, was and is great.

True greatness is measured not just by effect, but also time and extent. True greatness reaches beyond and above its immediate sphere of influence.

Phelps has changed nothing but a few world records in a pool – and possibly the value of stock for the Speedo swimsuit company. Ali changed the world.

Why does all of this matter?

Because what we are, who we are, what we think and do, ripples this pond we call "life." We should do our best to contribute, positively, to the extent of our gifts, and beyond. Hopefully our strivings make the world a better place.

Those who do should be celebrated.

I've Got a Sweetheart, and I Don't Care Who Knows

This time next week, I'll be in Arkansas visiting my sweetheart.

Don't worry, I have nothing hide from my wife. She knows all about the extra-special person in my life, whose love for me predated even her own. She's not jealous at all – though, sometimes, my mother is, when it comes to this "other woman".

Neither wife nor mother has anything to worry about. But they should also never expect to take this love's unique place in my heart.

They have loved me. But she has loved me, grandly.

My grandmother, my first "special sweetheart," turns 80 this month and most of the family – eight children, and scores and scads of grandchildren and great-grandchildren – are gathering to celebrate her milestone.

This will be a momentous trip for many reasons.

There is the crazy adventure of making a 12-hours-straight-through-and-12-hours-back whirlwind tour of Illinois, Missouri and the home of President Clinton.

And of course we'll see relatives on my mother's side that we haven't seen or talked with for years. We'll have to cram weeks, months, years of catching up into two short days.

But most of all, I'll get to see my grandmother again. Talking on the phone every few months is fine. And, given the realities of our lives, those brief conversations, usually around the holidays, must suffice. So any opportunity to actually see her, hug her, laugh and chat together, is to be cherished.

Many people have a special bond with a grandparent or grandparents. My own relationship is doubly blessed because I am the first grandchild, the eldest of the eldest of my grandmother's nine children. The next one, my middle brother Tim, didn't come along 16 months later.

So, for at least those 16 months, I reigned supreme on the "Grandchild List." I was it. The only, and most special – if merely by default (though I choose to believe it was by divine design...)

My grandmother was and, I am sure, still is a wonderful grandparent to all of her grandchildren. But I think that head start, that extra time together gave us something special.

Here's a silly, but telling example of our unique relationship: she'd hand-make pies for me whenever I'd ask. I prefer pie over cake any day, and my grandma's seemed to be better than anything anyone else ever made.

Later, my mother found out that my grandma actually used frozen pie crusts. She divulged this information in a fit of pique, as if she had discovered Amelia Earhart's remains in the back of my grandma's freezer.

Of course, my mother's outrage at this bit of deception completely missed the point. More important than where the pies came from, was who made them.

Later in life, facing a serious financial hurdle early in my young adulthood, I turned to my grandmother for help. I fretted for weeks before suffering the embarrassing discomfort to ask her for a small loan. She waited only as long as it took me to explain the situation to say yes.

And, at my father's funeral, she again came to my rescue when cracks of rifle fire shocked me out of my robotic emotionless state.

Standing at the graveside on a bitter, cold January day, I began sobbing as the 21-gun salute was made – the first tears I had cried since those I shed a few days before over his dead body lying exposed and cold on a hospital table.

I turned and reached for someone as my eyes and throat swelled. She was there. Coincidence? I think not.

I cried, and she held me like the 31-year-old baby I needed to be at that moment.

These are mere snippets of a lifelong love story that would take far too long to tell. And most of it would mean nothing to the reader who has no point of reference, nothing against which to measure the greatness of this woman's heart. Quiet conversations. Private assurances. Even a few firm corrections. (Not even Grandma thinks I am perfect.)

Her life has not been defined by any particular achievement, save that of simple survival – which is never as simple as it seems. Two husbands, eight children, and more ups and downs than a Rocky Mountain road trip.

Her tale, if ever told, would be a testament to the

power of pure gumption, courage, will, and love for those around her. In a world so often soured by cowardliness, cynicism and sadness, that's plenty. That's enough.

Grandma, you have shared a lifetime with a line of people too long to even count. I am grateful beyond measure for what you've given me. And, on this, your 80th birthday, I am proud and humbled and blessed to be somewhere near the front of that line as your first grandchild.

It may not mean much to anyone else. But to me, it'll always mean the world.

Like, the Art of Conversation, Like, Is, Like So Important

Honest to goodness, I thought my ears were going to bleed.

Sitting in the front seat of our van, chauffeuring our eldest daughter and her best friend to a movie, it seemed like someone had deposited a bank of rock band speakers in the back seat, or that a battalion of bees had broken through the glass.

I checked the rear-view mirror, afraid for what might appear.

Nope, just two teenage girls, chit-chat-chit-chattering away.

I was consoled. Yet also strangely frightened, knowing that I face at least three more years of similar endurance tests, as we continue to provide taxi services to both of our daughters…

I have blasted away at text messaging as the preferred communications mode for today's youth.

It occurs to me now that the problem with today's youthful communications may not be the vehicle of communications per se, as much as the communications themselves.

In the 40-or-so minutes that I shepherded those two 15-year-olds to and from the movie theater, I heard at least 30 different thoughts fired, like verbal buckshot.

Not one relevant string stretched beyond 20 words. And 15 of those words were "like."

Teenage girls have mastered the art of saying everything and nothing at the same time. My head was spinning at the gush of information. It was exhilarating and exhausting just listening to it, much less trying to follow along.

Boyfriends. School work. Teachers that they like and don't like. Work plans. Babysitting. Colleges that they want to attend. Rehashed telephone conversations. Stories about their siblings and parents and family members and friends and trips they've taken and, and, and, and...

It was as if the world would collapse if they didn't fill every miniscule fragment of space with sound.

And all (like) interspersed (like) with (like) giggles (like).

Please understand.

As the father of girls, and surrounded by strong, bright, talented, clever and extroverted women in every facet of my life, I do not want nor never intend to quash their spirits.

The only thing worse than a chatty teenage girl, is a sullen, withdrawn teenage girl. The kind who hates her siblings. Hates her parents. Hates school. Hates life.

The kind who wears black baggy pants and black eye makeup and a black scowl to show her blackened heart filled with disgust with and contempt for with the world around her.

There are plenty of those girls – and boys, for that matter – in the world today. Just check out any middle or high school.

And I also don't mean to suggest that teenage boys are any better communicators – if you call inarticulate grunting and monosyllabic, one-word responses "communications" at all.

My wife and I survived an entire summer of socializing between our daughters and their "boyfriends" – coincidentally, two brothers themselves the same age as our girls.

We are a social family. We enjoy each other's company and that of a circle of close friends and relatives.

Even I, the least social of all, like entertaining once I've had time (or my darling wife has pushed me, as only wives can) to warm up to the idea of others invading my personal space. Ironically, I usually end up being the center of attention somehow, the "featured clown."

So it was notably frustrating when we tried, almost daily, to engage those boys in something resembling conversation and rarely got anything beyond "Uh-huh" in response.

They weren't rude or disrespectful. They just didn't talk to us, beyond the basic social requirements of acknowledging their girlfriends' parents.

The silence was deafening – and irritating.

Thankfully, our daughters are confident, complex, creative young women who are, mostly, comfortable in their own skins.

We have and do read with them, encourage them to

read themselves, and teach them how to understand what they've read. Books, magazines, newspapers, the Internet. Anything and everything. The written word is sacrosanct. The purest and best vessel of ideas, intellect, knowledge and human progress.

It is OK in our house to ask, question, doubt. There are no sacred cows at our dinner table. Everything is open for respectful questioning – except the unquestionable fact that Mom and Dad are in charge.

As a family we try to include them in conversations, where appropriate. We talk with them and to them.

We treat them as if they actually have brains capable of taking in (if not always fully understanding) the world around them, and formulating opinions about same. So that they know that their contributions are valued, and valuable.

Honestly, this approach has not always worked as hoped.

We occasionally have to tell both girls to butt-out of certain conversations. Remind them that they are more "old children" than "young adults." And tell them to not repeat certain words or notions uttered by the sometimes-irresponsible adults around them, including us.

Still, I'd much rather have children who express themselves any day (even if that expression is teenage girl blather). Because children who communicate, become adults who communicate.

The ability to think, to analyze, and to communicate sets us apart from the animals. That, and the opposable thumb, are all that save us.

<u>Slugs, Grubs and Worms – Oh My!</u>

I am a born sucker for lists.

David Letterman is one of my longtime idols, not merely because of his scathing and fearless sense of humor and his place as the true and best replacement for the greatest of all nighttime television hosts, Johnny Carson.

I also love Letterman because of his wonderful, witty "Top 10" compilations. Likewise, all of those "Top 25 All-Time (insert your subject here)" lists of great movies, songs, books, etc. are surefire flames for my intellectual moth.

Along those lines, several years ago I subscribed to a magazine called "The Sun." It was a monthly literary publication which seemed right up my alley. It turned out to be more highfalutin than highbrow, however. I lost interest when it came time to re-up.

But each issue did include a feature called "10 Things" – seemingly-random thoughts about a particular topic that were, often very cleverly and subtly, connected.

I spent the better part of the last weekend trying to reclaim my yard and gardens after two weeks of vacation.

Maybe it was the sun's scorching impact on my brain. But, as I pulled the millionth weed, sweating so much that a pig would have run the other way, squealing in protest, to escape the smell, the thought occurred: gardening is a great big metaphor for life.

So, without promising to be either highfalutin or highbrow (or entertaining, for that matter), here are "10 Ways that Gardening Is like Life."

1. **Destruction comes a lot faster than construction.** We've been working, diligently, since early spring to cultivate and maintain our little corner of the world. Planting plants, pulling weeds, trimming trees, etc. But a mere two weeks away, and the place looked like the gardening equivalent of a war zone.

2. **Tomatoes usually taste better fresh off the vine.** Life is almost always better when it is lived simply, directly and without flashy garnish.

3. **It takes a lot of hard work to make a garden grow.** Hellooooo, everyone who feels that life owes you something for nothing... Sometimes you have to bend down, dig around and get some dirt under your nails to see good results. Your back and knees will ache. But the pain will seem worth it later, sitting on your patio with a cold beer or iced tea, admiring the fruits (and vegetables) of your labor.

4. **A good plan will solve many problems.** "Plan" is not a four-letter word. Take some time before

planting to think things through, read up on the best practices, anticipate challenges and details, learn from someone who knows a little more. This prep work will result in beautiful arrays all season long, rather than a flame of color that burns out after July 4th.

5. **On the other hand, understand that you can't plan for everything.** Sometimes, despite our best forward-thinking efforts, weeds happen. Deal with it. Don't whine. It's ugly and unproductive.

6. **Speaking of which: weeds are weeds only because someone decided that they are.** Someone, at some time, rather capriciously, decided that a rose is more favored than a dandelion. That this plant is more attractive than that one. That this one is "native" to a particular area. Hogwash. Plants grow wherever they can. Life is full of such arbitrary arrogance.

7. **Sometimes, that "magic fertilizer" is just expensive junk.** Often, the only thing that really grows when you use such products is the manufacturer's profit margin. Anything that assures success without hard work – whether a promise to produce 30-pound tomatoes or a get-rich-quick scheme – is usually a scam.

8. **Every garden, no matter how gorgeous, is full of gross, and sometimes painful, things.** Worms, grubs, snails, bugs, frogs, thorns, burrs, rabbits and other assorted critters. Hard as it may be, remember that they all play a part in the big picture, if only to remind us that life is equal parts pain and joy, beauty and ugliness. Especially as

you're digging another sliver from your thumb. Or stifling a scream of terror after some squishy thing hiding under a leaf unexpectedly moved when you touched it. Or wondering what in the world Mother Nature was thinking when she created something as disgusting as a slug.

9. **Death happens.** It's OK if your lawn turns brown from July through September. It'll come back in October, right on schedule. This dormancy period is nature's way of giving the grass a break and helping it prepare for winter. Death is a part of life, and life is about the long haul, not just the moment.

10. **Remember your place in the garden, and that there's always another hand at work.** We have a stone in our garden that says, "Nowhere on earth is one closer to God, than in the garden." A prescient (and decorative) reminder that we are smaller than we think, and that no amount of our hard work will ever top that which God does without breaking a sweat.

And if you don't believe that, then <u>you</u> go make a tree out of nothing...

Chaos, Clutter and a Contented Life

I recently squeezed yet another in the seemingly-endless parade of fall decorations onto an already-overcrowded shelf in my garage.

And as I fought the battle for space, the thought occurred that my life is a lot like my garage after 11.5 years in what was (and still is) our first house.

Mostly clean, but dirty in the corners. Oil spotting the floor here and there. Not nearly as spacious as would have expected by this point. Cluttered with stuff, much of which isn't mine, some of which I'd throw away if I had my druthers.

It's probably no coincidence that this barrage of reflective bombs came screaming at me within weeks of my 42 birthday. I know in my heart of hearts that 42 isn't all that old. It's the leading edge of middle age. Just one more step along life's long road.

Yet, I'm having some trouble believing my heart of hearts largely because my body of bodies is in painful cahoots with my mind of minds.

Nothing like sore feet, aching knees, a tender back, diminishing vision, an ever-expanding waist line, puffy jowls and graying hair to really make one feel good about his place in the physical world.

And even when I come to grips with all of that, I still run headlong into a life full of "stuff" that makes even a hairline receding at the speed of light seem like a minor irritation.

There are the financial challenges that I never would have expected at this age. The family issues that should have resolved themselves many years ago. The professional hurdles that time and experience should have cleared by now.

I mean, shouldn't I have been further along? Didn't my early adolescence foretell much more promise than my current station in life suggests? Did I miss an important fork in the road somewhere? Or worse, did I knowingly take a wrong tong?

Not to mention the rigors of living with teenagers – and girls, to boot – that no pre-teen dose of "I'm telling you it's only going to get worse" rhetoric, no matter how much, no matter how sincere, could have prepared me for.

And please understand, even as I write that last paragraph, I know that mine are good kids.

I cannot even imagine what I would do if I had to deal with some of the children I regularly encounter. The disrespect. The bad behavior and poor manners. The purposeful derision of and disregard for anything that does not center precisely on them. Suffice to say, there might be a few less teenagers in the world.

So there I stood in my garage, my feeble brain cells

firing like pistons in an engine desperately in need of a tune-up, making these random, self-pitying connections.

Then I looked around again (after shoving one more ceramic frog between the layers of cushions from the outdoor furniture.) I don't know, I may have hit my head on the handlebars of my daughter's bike hanging overhead, because my vision changed. Another thought occurred:

Sure my garage is cluttered. But at least I have a garage.

And it's attached to a house.

And in that house are the four people (counting the dog) who define my own existence, who mean more to me than anyone, or anything in the world.

And from that garage, we live our lives as a family. We come and go and do, together. To school, birthday parties, work, church, community functions.

That garage holds the lawn mower and snow blower that help us keep our little corner of the world safe and attractive. It holds seeds that give us beauty and food, the baseball gloves and balls and bats that keep us amused, and the camping gear that gives us hope, in the deepest, darkest days of winter.

It may be unintentionally chaotic, the floors spotty and the corners in need of a good sweeping. But that garage, like life, is just what we made it, and just what it is supposed to be.

Less is More; Less is Enough

It was a good weekend for friends.

If the world ended today, would you regret not spending another hour at the office, cutting grass, cleaning windows, folding laundry, pulling weeds, tidying the garage, asphalting the driveway, or any of the scores of tasks that chip away at our lives, one dull-edged chore at a time?

Probably not.

But most of us would miss the opportunity to spend a few hours with family and friends.

To share a bottle of wine over a good meal. To celebrate the impending birth of another baby. To worship our God together. To enjoy a new CD or an old movie. To take a Sunday afternoon nap – virtually unheard of today.

To ride a bike or toss a ball (or both) with our children. To read a few pages in a good book. To snuggle in bed, tired but (for the first time in many months) not exhausted.

These are simple things. But that unfettered simplicity is their magic. Their charm. Their incalculable value.

That was our weekend.

My wife – it is such an understatement to call her my better half that it borders on insulting – invited two couples to whom we are very close, for dinner.

Seeing as how she is a professional chef, rarely does anyone turn down the chance to partake of my wife's vittles.

In this case, however, one couple, Paul and Mary Ellen, could not make it. This actually was not a bad thing. Paul has been extremely sick for several months. In the hospital, intensive care, facing death (at least temporarily), out of work, the whole nine yards.

However they couldn't make it because they were leaving for a short vacation – he was finally well enough to endure travel – which came as very welcome news. We love them. We missed them. But we couldn't be happier that they were absent.

But Jeff and Maxine, parents of our godchildren, rang the door bell promptly at 5 p.m. Saturday.

Maxine is pregnant with their third daughter. A very bright, strong, and charming woman under any circumstances, pregnancy has made her even more beautiful than usual.

Jeff is, simply, great. I don't have many close male friends. Jeff is about it. Kind, patient, deviously, deceptively funny.

They make for great dinner company. The kind of people you hope will always number high on your list of lifelong companions. The kind of friends who are more like family than some actual family.

Later, sleeping in Sunday morning seemed like a great idea.

Then the phone rang. It was Sandy. An old friend whose son was our eldest daughter's first "boyfriend" when they were both five. You get the point: their very short-lived love affair was more a bonding for us as parents than for them (thank goodness) as children.

She and her second husband and their kids moved away a few years ago.

But my wife and Sandy have kept in touch. Since moving, Sandy -- a vivacious woman with a personality so sparkling that champagne seems flat by comparison -- divorced her second husband, remarried, divorced again, and is now working on reconciling with former-hubby number three.

Sandy and her former/current/future (?) man invited us to church. They attend a Baptist church. We'd never attended a Baptist church, so we said yes, partly for the adventure of trying something new as well as for the opportunity to meet up with our old friend.

And a faith adventure it was for us Lutherans and former Catholics who are used to a slightly more somber, reflective atmosphere. But certainly an experience worth having, and perhaps repeating.

We all need a break now and again. A reminder that there's more to life than the glare and noise and electricity we vainly generate and inhabit and endure to try to give meaning and value and purpose to our lives.

And as is so often the case in life, less is more. Less glare, less noise, less electricity. Sometimes, the truest meaning and value and purpose come through the time shared with friends.

And that's more than enough.

Free Steak, Free Cake and Freedom

I was actually put off steak.

My first real job, the first for which my pay came from someone not related to me, the first for which I had to use my social security number, was as the morning clean-up person at the old Ponderosa Steakhouse in Joliet.

Each morning that summer of my 15th year, my dad – who, of course, helped get me the job, since he, as a Will County Sheriff's deputy, knew the manager -- would drive me to the restaurant.

Each morning I would clean the grills. No easy task for someone who, even then, didn't like getting dirty. Grease, small bits of charred meat, and other nauseating flotsam greeted me each day, gross and disgusting partners with the summer sunshine.

Then I'd vacuum the entire restaurant, amazed at what people would leave behind. Bits of bread, salad from the then-revolutionary salad bar, napkins and (again!) meat scraps created their own counter-pattern in the carpet. The night clean-up crew either was blind as a cave of bats, or sadistically enjoyed leaving the mess for the teenager coming in the morning.

Finally, I'd help out a bit with the lunchtime crowd, bussing tables and running the register until my ride home arrived.

One of the benefits of this job was that employees could eat free.

So, as you'd expect for someone raised on a chicken budget, I'd have steak for lunch.

Seemed like a great idea at the time. Free food? Great! Go for the good stuff! But too much if a good thing, as the saying goes, can become a bad thing.

By the time I severed ties with the restaurant, I couldn't eat steak if the choice were that or a bullet to the brain. To this day, steak, while certainly good, does not ring my culinary bells.

This memory butterfly-ed recently through my aging and addled brain as I dropped my eldest – herself 15 – off at her first real job.

With official work permit in hand, she applied for and was hired to be the weekend front counter and clean-up person at Cathy's Sweet Creations bakery.

The owner is a dear family friend. But to her everlasting credit, she made my daughter go through the entire job hunting process just as if she were Anonymous Applicant #223. No free passes here.

She completed the application, endured an interview, and waited several days before learning that she was hired. Subsequently, with mom and dad's help, she filled out her tax withholding forms and the usual passel of paperwork.

She's been babysitting for a couple of years now. And,

frankly, knowing some of the babies she sits for, I know for certain that watching them is at least as challenging as working at the bakery.

But this is different.

Ones first real, paying job is usually ones first foray into the adult world. The first wobbly/gleeful steps toward independence.

Of course, after her first two weekends as a real working gal, our daughter is ecstatic. Tired, but ecstatic.

And of course, I am heartbroken.

Because each of these steps forward in life is taken on stiletto heels standing on my toes. Sharp, blade-like stiletto heels, strapped to the feet of a young woman – no longer a child, though still my baby. Each step towards adulthood is another away from Mom and Dad.

Don't get me wrong.

I am happy for our eldest daughter. Likewise I am happy for our youngest who now has a chance to shine a little brighter, out a bit from her sister's encompassing shadow. And she's a real popper and show stopper in her own right.

Still, progress always comes at a cost. In this case, the cost is merely, but significantly emotional, and no less rending for its inevitability.

In a few days, our daughter will bring home her first paycheck. It will probably be for less than $100. But for her, just as it is for everyone, it will be like holding a handful of gold.

Though her mom and I still have to drive her everywhere, she is now on the road to real life.

Later, hopefully much later, she, like many adults, may come to see that paycheck as a tie that binds – to mortgages, car payments and assorted other forms of slavery-disguised-as-life.

Working may not always be as exciting for her as it is now. Holding down a job usually loses some of its luster when it becomes a "have to" rather than a "want to."

But today, she is gainfully and happily employed. And, knowing her, she will never tire of eating bakery goodies.

The First "First"

Well Emma, you've hit it squarely on the head.

That no longer surprises me, though you're only 5. As your father, I admit that I like to fool myself into thinking that I know everything about you. But as you've grown up, I have often been amazed by your depth of perception and sensitivity to other people's feelings.

Now, I almost expect you – and others of your generation – to understand certain things about life and people through an intuition that I either never had, or which has been dulled by the cynicism that comes with age.

So when I chuckled at your recent solemn pronouncement that you were "a little bit nervous" about your first day of kindergarten, I wasn't laughing at you. I wasn't even laughing at the statement itself. After all, you've said lots of things that at first led me to vainly believe my oldest child was a genius, only to concede (if only privately) that you were probably parroting something you'd overheard.

It wasn't the words themselves that caught me off guard, but the sincerity behind them. It seemed that you had somehow sensed my own misgivings as you took the next Big Step toward the rest of your life.

Don't get me wrong, Emma. As your dad, I was very happy for you and proud as you started kindergarten, and I know you will do well in school, because you've been looking forward to it for so long.

I remember your excited squeals as a toddler every time the sunshine-colored bus passed outside our little apartment window, carting a load of rollicking children to the nearby elementary school.

Sometimes we could even hear the kids laughing and screaming on those buses when the weather was warm enough for the children to open the windows, and you would ask when you could go to school "like the big kids." The thought of all the adventures that school brings lit up your face like a fireplace on Christmas Eve.

But, as an adult familiar with the harder edges of "real life," I also am a little scared for you, knowing what is ahead.

Sure, there will be many moments of elation and exciting "firsts."

The first time you read a book all by yourself, or correctly calculate the number of animals Farmer Jones has will undoubtedly and rightly leave you bursting with pride. Your first school play will bring so much excitement that you probably won't be able to remember your lines.

Your first report card, dance, sleepover, musical concert, choral recital, athletic event, field trip, even (heaven save me) your first little "boyfriend," among the many experiences that only school can bring, will be as thrilling for your mom and me as they will be for you.

What concerns me, though, is the other stuff that also comes with this official entrée into the world as it (unfortunately) really is.

The first time another child teases you because of your (pick one): new hairstyle, shoes, eyes, backpack, lunch or any of the other myriad list of silly, ultimately meaningless things that kids pick on other kids about, will leave me as broken-hearted as I am sure you will be.

Painful confusion will follow the first time some friend abandons you to buddy up with someone deemed "cooler." You will no doubt come home one day (hopefully, much later than kindergarten or even elementary school) and cry to me or your mom about your boyfriend breaking up with you.

And further down the road there will be the predictably, inevitable yet incredibly maddening teen-parent rift, as you decide, despite our lifetime of devotion and caring, that you don't want your parents around when you're with your friends.

Certainly, we'll mend those wounds because we love you as only parents can. But when the time comes, I know those fights will bring hurt like nothing short of a ripping knife to the gut.

When these things happen, you might ask how I knew that they would. It's not that I'm psychic. Rather, my insight, like most parents, comes from something more sharply, tangibly humbling: experience.

The school door is the first true portal to Real Life.

Blanketed by a family's love, life is usually rich and filled with joy. But, it can also be harsh and difficult. And reality won't let you escape life, anymore than it will let me protect you from it, no matter how much I may want to, or try.

And that makes me "a little bit nervous."

Elvis: The Once and Future King

My good friend Don was there.

So was his wife, Tammera, and Brenda and Mike and their kids. And Michele and Tim, all terrific friends, and my wife, Kellie and our daughters, and a bunch of people I didn't even know.

We were all there at Steve and Gina Costello's house, on an amazing, this-is-what-it's-supposed-to-be-like-on-June-20th Friday night.

And we all saw Elvis.

Not only did we see him, but we watched him open birthday presents (funniest darned thing you ever saw,) eat birthday cake off the ground (he wasn't supposed to) and snuffle like a pig desperate for a decongestant in his mother's arms (strange, but true.)

Elvis is Steve and Gina's dog. Yes, his full name is Elvis Costello. No, there is no pun or joke intended.

Every year the Costellos, who are very good friends of ours, throw Elvis a birthday party. What better reason to gather good friends and family on a late spring evening than to watch a Boston Terrier rip open his own birthday presents?

Friends. Family. Faith. The three "F's" that make the world go around, and the way they mix to create the kind of fun that is both exciting and calming. They remind us of the way things should be.

That's the secret to a good life.

Not money, nor fame, nor power.

We'll leave the politics, local and global, packed away for another week. There will always be politics and taxes and development and the economy and all those other issues that complicate our lives.

But there won't always be a picture perfect June night on which friends, old and new, gathered on the "what more excuse do we need?" premise of celebrating a dog's birthday.

And so it is those moments that have to be commemorated and celebrated. Because they are rare and special in world sadly overflowing with issues and problems and concerns and difficulties.

Do we have enough money for the bills this month? Will our community ever find enough space in our schools for all of the kids who keep coming? Will our state make it through this financial crisis? Will our country ever find those weapons of mass destruction? Will the world ever learn to just get along?

Who cares?

For this one night it was all about Elvis's birthday.

Then again, it's not about Elvis's birthday. You pick your occasion.

You decide what will be your chance to just forget about all of your daily dilemmas, reach out to some friends, smile over a drink or a bratwurst, laugh at how kids who, moments ago didn't know each other, but always seem to find a way to quickly become fast friends.

Take that opportunity when it comes. And for those few, precious moments, let everything else slip away.

And through it all runs the gift of faith.

That these people are good people. That they have no malicious intent, no political agenda, no designs on your time other than to love and share their own happiness.

And most of all, faith that the God who put us all here, giving us a place and time to be together, meant to do so. This is part of His big plan. He means for us to know each other as friends and family.

We should be able to enjoy time with friends without fearing that doing so means the lawn won't get cut, or that we won't be able to work more overtime to fill this month's financial gap.

We should be able to take the time to watch our children grow. Who needs 57 channels and 35 varieties of "reality television" when we can watch, for free, the coolest reality show of all -- our offspring learning who they are as they become what they will become.

Best of all, we get to play along, if we choose. And the rewards are worth far more than what those self-embarrassing nitwits get on any of those so-called "reality shows."

We should be able to take a break from the world's ills without feeling that somehow, someway, our leisure is contributing to the problems.

Some of us, myself included, often waste more energy by erecting hurdles to deny ourselves life's simple pleasures than we would ever spend simply enjoying them. "There's too much to do," we whine. "I'm too busy," we cry.

But no more. Elvis reminded me of a basic, essential lesson. Life is for living.

Thanks, Elvis. You remain The King.

Speaking the Eternal Truth

I have a dream.

Dr. Martin Luther King Jr.'s "Dream," actually.

It has long been my ambition to deliver Dr. King's monumental "I Have a Dream" speech to some group. Any group. Indeed, the identity or size or composition of the group doesn't matter nearly as much as the opportunity to speak the words that Dr. King spoke on August 28, 1963.

That goal came back to me recently when I Dr, King's birthday holiday afforded me the blessing of a day off following several very challenging and draining weeks.

Then with some shame for my selfishness, it quickly occurred that the real blessing of the day is the opportunity to remember Dr. King's birthday and honor his memory and how his work on behalf of African Americans benefited all citizens.

Dr. King was many things, positive and negative. Both his supporters and critics have wide platforms on which to stand.

But above all he was a brilliant thinker, writer and speaker.

I do a lot of public speaking both personally and professionally. I'm pretty good at it. Even my worst critics – of which there are myriad – agree. And yet, on my best, best, best day, I couldn't begin to approach Dr. King's oratory magic.

It's also fair to say that I can string together a decent sentence. But nothing I am ever likely to write will compare to Dr. King's worst throw-away rhetoric.

Some would say that the difference is the times that Dr. King lived in, and the subject matter he addressed. He spent much of his adult life addressing the felonious treatment of an entire people – free, patriotic American citizens robbed of the very rights that even the worst criminals are guaranteed, and for better reason than the color of their skin.

Yet, I believe that Dr. King could have written and spoken magnificently on any subject in any given time. Because the brilliance of his words did not come from his pen, but from him. The coals of his passion fired everything he did and made him an engine of civic discourse.

The real strength of Dr. King's words is that they still ring true today. What he said then remains powerful and true because his message addressed the human condition, not just the condition of the humans of his day.

He wrote about the "promissory note to which every American was to fall heir," and how "America has defaulted on this promissory note," for the African Americans of his day.

Yet those words apply just as well today to any group

suffering from oppression, hatred, short-sightedness and fear – Muslims, gays, and anyone who speaks, thinks or looks different than the majority.

Optimistically, Dr. King went on say "We refuse to believe that the bank of justice is bankrupt."

We continue to believe – or, at least, we better – that the promise of justice will always define and preserve this country or America will collapse and crumble under the weight of its inherent fractious nature.

On the subject of debate and protest, Dr. King balanced the urge for physical response with the need for personal responsibility:

"We must forever conduct our struggle on the high plane of dignity and discipline. We must not allow our creative protest to degenerate into physical violence. Again and again we must rise to the majestic heights of meeting physical force with soul force."

Now as then, tomorrow as yesterday, the heart, the mind, the spirit are better tools for discourse and disagreement than the fist.

At the root of his dream, Dr. King planted a vision: that "one day every valley shall be exalted, every hill and mountain shall be made low, the rough places will be made plain, and the crooked places will be made straight, and the glory of the Lord shall be revealed, and all flesh shall see it together."

Not black flesh or white flesh or old flesh or young flesh or straight flesh or gay flesh or Christian flesh or Muslim flesh. All flesh.

And nothing remains truer today, as we continue to fight a war supposedly to give freedom to another people even as our own freedoms are threatened, than Dr. King's assertion that we will never be free, until we are all free:

"And when this happens, when we allow freedom to ring, when we let it ring from every village and every hamlet, from every state and every city, we will be able to speed up that day when all of God's children, black men and white men, Jews and Gentiles, Protestants and Catholics, will be able to join hands and sing in the words of the old Negro spiritual, 'Free at last, free at last! Thanks God almighty, we are free at last!"

No one, yesterday or today, could have ever said it better.

Signs, Signs, Everywhere There Are Signs

Consider this fair warning: Stay off the road if I'm on it – especially if driving on said road involves any signage.

Well, not any signage, exactly. But apparently I have some problems recognizing a few important signs -- five, to be exact.

I learned of this critical defect in my knowledge set when I went to renew my driver's license. Turns out that it was my turn to take the written test.

Near as I can remember, I haven't taken a written driving test since I got my license 26 years ago. However, I have been driving for all of those 26 years.

Now, I've had my share of driving accidents and incidents, but none of them because I misunderstood or ignored a road sign. So you would have thought that life experience on the road would have more than compensated for lack of experience on the test.

Wrong-a-rooni!

I did very well on the written portion of the test. Missed only one question. In reality, no one should do poorly on the questions. They're written in such a way that they almost shout the correct answer. Something like:

"If you are sitting at an intersection and a sweet, blue-haired woman is toddling slowly across the street right in front of your car, do you

A) Rev the engine to scare the living daylights out of her?

B) Lay on the horn to see if she keels over?

C) Scream obscenities out the window about how she should go die somewhere else, or

D) Wait patiently for her to cross, understanding that pedestrians have the same rights as drivers?"

The next section shows about 15 road signs. In my own defense, these are drawings, not pictures of actual signs. And, some of them did not include key markings or information. I guess the people who made the test must have felt that they'd already given the idiots taking it all the east answers that they could afford.

The test taker must choose an answer from a list and match it to the right sign. Seems simple enough, right? But nothing is ever as easy as it seems.

To make the test even more challenging, there were three more choices provided than there were signs. And somehow, they all seemed kinda-sorta correct.

I was fairly confident on most of the signs. Of course, I got the most important ones with no problem – for example, I knew right away that the red thing with eight sides, that's a stop sign. Hey, I is a college graduate!

But then I stumbled on the round yellow one (for railroad crossing); the orange rectangle (construction ahead); and the upside down triangle (either slow moving vehicles like a tractor, or that the vehicle is carrying toxic waste, or an indication that nuclear holocaust has taken place…I am still not sure about that one…)

The other two had nothing to do with everyday life – something about merging and passing lanes, I think…

Again, in my defense your honors – er, I mean, dear readers – none of those three signs included any other markings to clarify their meaning.

The yellow circle did not have on it the black "X" or the two "R's" that one typically associates with, you know, "railroad crossing." Nor did the orange rectangle show anyone with hard hats. I am sure that other bright, successful people might have missed them, too. I couldn't have been the only knucklehead, could I?

Anyway, standing at the counter, the person grading my test – a late-middle aged schoolmarm type -- took me to task for missing these signs, especially the railroad one which, she claimed, is the only yellow circular sign in Illinois.

"That's kind of ironic, since I live in Plainfield where 'railroads' should be our middle name," I replied with a chuckle. She was not amused.

And to really rub road salt into the wounds, coming back from the license facility I must have passed 50 construction signs. I saw so much orange that I thought I had somehow driven into a pumpkin patch.

In the end, getting six questions wrong – including five road signs – still allowed me to drive in Illinois. You can decide if that's good news or bad, and plan your own driving accordingly.

As for me, I have a license for four more years. Since we plan to stay in Plainfield for at least that long, that works out to approximately 8,486,352 more sightings of railroad crossing and construction signs.

And, more importantly, it gives me four more years to figure out what in the world that inverted triangle means.

Ah! I know! "Vehicle carrying pineapple upside down cake."

Everywhere You Look, the Same, Same, Same

America is built on the ideals of tolerance, respect and appreciation of difference. At least in theory, if not always in practice.

The belief that everyone is created equal and is endowed with certain basic rights, no matter where we come from or look like or what language we speak or religion we practice. This is the very cornerstone of our American social and political system. There is no more solid foundation on which to build a community.

Yet, that foundation, lies on shifting sands.

We are also, by definition, by design, by default, a nation of self contradiction. And it's wonderful! And infuriating!

These thoughts follow reading a wonderful short novel called "The Giver," by Lois Lowry, encouraged by my eldest daughter, who has in recent years become an avid bookworm.

Several times in the last few years she's recommended books written for young readers. Each time I scoff, thinking they couldn't possibly hold any interest for me, a middle-aged adult whose literary interests run toward the classics.

Each time, I've tripped over my arrogance, saved from bruising only by my deflated ego and over-padded butt. Important Life Lesson learned: Great ideas, insight, wisdom and inspirational communication are not the exclusive province of the old(er).

"The Giver" tells the story of a future society in which the leaders have removed anything that could create an air of "difference" or cause any kind of social division – color, music, language, behavior. The government provides an "ideal" community by controlling everything to ensure "sameness".

The leaders designate jobs for everyone in the society on their 12th birthdays. Spouses are assigned to each other. Most of them do not have children. Rather, children are provided to qualifying couples. (Everyone 12 and older takes pills to control their sexual urges.)

Those who misbehave are punished. Those who keep misbehaving are "released" from the community. So are the elderly after they're no longer useful, and any babies who weigh less than their "ideal" birth weight. (I'm not giving away too much by clarifying that "released" is a euphemism for euthanasia.)

All in the name of "sameness." Anything that could offend or hurt or disrupt has been, or is, contained, controlled, eliminated, to avoid disorder and chaos.

Including memories.

Only one person is allowed access to the community's memories. They must be protected for reference by the community leaders, but they cannot be shared with the community. Too much pain, temptation, confusion, and, possibly, turmoil would result.

That person is the only one who knows, through the community's memories, the anguish of starvation, the horror of war, the loss of death.

Yet, he's also the only one to know the euphoria of love, the warmth of sunshine, the exhilaration of a sled ride, the thrill of music, the completing joy of family. He must pass these memories to his designated replacement, a 12-year-old boy named Jonas. He is "The Giver" of the title.

It's a fascinating, disturbing, thought-provoking book, all the more intriguing for the ways it mirrors our own world.

We move toward dangerous "sameness" -- in ways big and small, overt and covert, political, social, religious, economical, communal -- every time we withhold respect, dignity and basic rights from people we disagree with.

They don't look like us. They don't talk like us. They don't behave like us. So they don't deserve the same rights as us. Whichever "us" happens to be in power at the time.

Slaves, women, homosexuals, Muslims, every immigrant population that's ever crossed America's threshold, have all fallen victim to our strange and ironic American urge toward "sameness."

This is the case every time we criticize people who don't speak English – as if the ability to speak English is a defining measure of ones value.

Ironically, English is a linguistic bastard, a mish-mash of most of the world's tongues. Why, if it weren't for Irish, Italian, French, Spanish and the many other languages from which we've stolen, the English dictionary would weigh about 4 ounces.

Every time we ridicule and dismiss another religious system besides that which defines our own relationship with and understanding of God – or lack thereof.

Starting with all of the variations of Christianity, moving through Judaism, Islam, Hinduism, nature cults and Wiccans, and coming full circle with agnostics and atheists, everyone is entitled to his or her own spiritual connections. This bit of discrimination is, perhaps, the silliest of all. In the end, no one who is still breathing can know which religious system has it right.

America is built on the idea that we're all entitled to be who we are, and as different as we want to be, so long as your "being" doesn't threaten or hurt mine.

True freedom is a concept as realistically challenging as it is philosophically beautiful. It has absolutely nothing to do with "sameness."

By definition, it must be shared with and applied to everyone, even – especially – those we don't like. Diversity emboldens freedom. It makes us a better, stronger people. Embrace diversity. Embrace freedom.

As The Giver might say, "how sad it would be if we were all the same."

As Long As You Live Under My Roof…

It remains some of the best advice I've ever received.

Though it came years before we became parents, it addressed parenting.

Somewhat poetic, the advice was proffered in a conversation whose larger context and content I no longer remember. It isn't nearly as important as that one blurb that sticks with me to this day:

"Be their friend later. Be their parent now."

Time and again, this gem of wisdom has flashed inside my head like a neon sign on an eternal timer. It's always triggered by yet another example of indulgent, irresponsible, short-sighted parenting – which never seems to be in short supply.

Times have changed. Laws have been written to protect our children from abuse. That's good. But as with many things in our media-centric culture, what was created with good intentions has been taken too far.

Now anyone with a cell phone is prepped and primed to video any kind of physical contact and turn it over to the first television station willing to pay them a few bucks, as an example of discipline gone bad.

Kids think that they can press charges if their parents dare to raise their voice or, heaven forbid, raise a hand, to discipline them.

But simple, basic parental discipline is far from criminal. And, quite to the contrary, the lack of parental discipline should indeed be criminal for the damage it does.

Firm, loving discipline is essential to raising responsible functioning children.

So that they will learn appropriate social decorum.

So that they don't think the world owes them everything just because they draw air into their lungs.

So that they behave correctly in the home, in school, in life.

So that they don't cause unnecessary problems for themselves, their parents, their families and society.

You know the age-old question, "What's wrong with kids today"? The answer, in a lot of cases, is "their parents".

Parents who shirk this responsibility, either because of some ill-advised effort to "let their children learn on their own." Or to not hamper their free spirit. Or because they "can't control them." Or, worst of all, they want their children to think of them as their friends.

Instead of asking, "what can I do about it," parents need to be the adult in the relationship.

How about explaining the idea of social and cultural context – that sometimes there are rules that, while inconvenient to the child, are important in the "big picture." And, that sometimes the "big picture" must take precedence over individual wants.

Please notice that I didn't say "needs" – as is often the case in today's world, this issue is not one of necessity or sustenance, but rather singular self expression.

Oh, and here's a novel concept: explain, firmly but lovingly, that a child does not have the right to dictate what he or she will do as long as he or she is still eating the food and living under the roof that the parent provides.

Parenting is hard work, Lord knows. It demands the courage to say "no," so that later on, children will know when "yes" is the right answer.

It requires love them enough to allow them to hate you now, in trade for understanding and, maybe if you're lucky, appreciation later.

It demands teaching and insisting on respect, so that they will earn and deserve respect themselves as they grow.

And we do this, not because we want to make our children's lives miserable – though they may think so at least for a while – but because we dare to want for them the best life possible.

To be fair, nothing in life is as black and white as it may seem in adulthood. Adolescence is defined by its dramas, traumas and extremes. It's only later, seen through the filter of experience that we realize how silly it all really was.

And, everyone has the right to his or her individualism. That's a bedrock tenet of American culture, such as it is.

But, in the real world, sometimes life isn't easy.

Sometimes there are bumps in the road. Sometimes we just can't have everything we want. Acknowledging and teaching as much to our children is not defeat. That's discipline. That's not resignation. That's maturity.

We must love our children enough to help them understand this while we still have some access and control as their parents.

Then, we can laugh about it later, together, as friends.

It Takes a Licking, and Keeps on Ticking

My dad's watch is dying.

It's not fancy. No depth meter. No star charts. No telling time in foreign countries. No exotic leather band. Just a basic timepiece. Simple, unaffected, solid, reliable. Like him.

It is also my favorite memento of his, acquired after he died. My mother divided up those possessions of his that she was willing to part with between my brothers and me.

I am not particularly sentimental, so I took only a few things. One of his police jackets, a gun holster, a hat. A shoulder patch from his uniform. A few smaller trinkets that I gave to my two daughters.

One not quite 3 and the other yet an infant when he died, they have only the vaguest memories of their Grandpa Tony, and really only those supplied through family folk lore.

But I kept his watch.

It's not that it held any particular place in my heart. I

didn't buy it for him nor did he leave it to me. I guess, for lack of any better reason, I took it because he wore it.

I've written many times about my dad and our unique relationship. Young, dashing Mexican man married young, attractive white woman coming out of a bad first marriage. Adopts her two infant sons, raises them as his own, etc. No need to dive back into that pool.

Except to say that, while I was his oldest son, his child by his choosing rather than by nature's chance, and loved him deeply and admired and respected him in many ways, my dad and I weren't, shall we say, always on the same page.

Politically, he couldn't have been more right-wing. Like most people of his generation -- and certainly like most cops of his time – he wore his biases and prejudices openly.

And there were plenty. Some were especially awkward, even embarrassing for an oldest son with several friends and acquaintances who didn't fit neatly into his dad's social box.

Musicians (long-haired hippies). Actors (gays). Critical thinkers and political liberals (rebels and trouble makers). People of color (words that cannot and should not be used).

Still, none of that mattered when I was the first to lay eyes on his father's dead body that January day in 1997.

He died of a heart attack at work. We both worked in downtown Chicago, so I was closest to the scene. Charged with officially identifying the body at the hospital, I nodded.

My duties done, alone in the room, I laid my head on his bare chest. Angry, crushed by the weight of a moment both inevitable and yet unimaginable and shocking when it actually arrives, I sobbed.

Then, I cared only that he was gone.

In my late 20s, we had finally started to connect, through my children. Finally had something in common – fatherhood – beyond our love of James Bond, John Wayne and the Chicago Bears.

So I took the watch, because it was the thing that had been closest thing to him. Literally and symbolically.

The watch has survived much over the last dozen years.

Besides the usual banging and clanging around, it was nearly lost when I took it off while working outside, put it over my car antenna so as to not forget it, and promptly forgot it. The watch remained on the antenna for a day or so.

I've had to replace the battery several times and the crystal once – though the jeweler couldn't find the exact match. So now, the watch is kind of a mixture of my dad and me, I suppose. At some point, I am not sure when, the crystal cracked slightly.

The band, one of those metallic twisty things, often pinches my skin or pulls the hair at my wrist. Sometimes it's too loose, sometimes too tight, depending on the season and the humidity.

While appropriate for business wear, it's not exactly the kind of watch one sports as a fashion statement or for fancy occasions. Not that I am inclined toward either.

Being a simple man at heart, it is one of only three pieces of jewelry that I wear. My wedding band and a silver "WWJD" bracelet, a birthday gift from my wife years ago, are the others.

But last week I noticed that the gears are slipping.

The day/date wheels keep stopping midway between, or don't turn at all, or, strangely, go backwards.

A battery and crystals are relatively inexpensive. Replacing or fixing watch gears, even on something as simple as this, will probably cost a lot more than the watch is worth.

Unless, that is, the "worth" is measured in something more valuable than money. Like memories.

Time keeps marching on. So will my watch.

The Lonely Dad Tango

I've seen my future. It seems I'll be dancing alone.

At least, I won't be boogying any large part of the night away with either of my daughters, if a recent Daddy-Daughter soiree was any indication of what tomorrow holds.

And I'll be honest. It breaks my heart.

The father of two Brownies, I have attended two Girl Scout Daddy-Daughter dances now. The first, last year, my eldest, Emma was my date. This year I briefly double dated with both Emma and my youngest, Olivia.

Always the tomboyish trooper, Olivia insisted on getting dolled up and going to the dance although she wasn't feeling well. But I eventually had to bring her home. So in all fairness, who knows? She may end up being my party partner for a long time.

But Emma, now two months shy of nine, is in full pre-teen posse mode. When I returned after taking Olivia home, Emma led me through the red and pink crepe paper streamers raining down over the entrance, a true vision in her formal finest.

We entered during a fast song. So it was a matter of seconds before I was standing on the dance floor alone, awkwardly trying to bop to the beat of some boy band's electronically-bolstered attempt at music. Meanwhile, my baby, my angel, my first proof of God ran into a pack of similarly-coifed, equally-squealing little girls.

I followed her into this ring of pre-teen beauties. Not wanting to look too desperate, but hoping that she'd remember that she had not driven there by herself, I took her hand and smiled.

Always the conscientious social butterfly, Emma quickly introduced me around. And then promptly turned away again to dance in a circle with her friends. I hit the pizza and pop, found a seat at a lunchroom table, and caught the eyes of several other dads also paddling one handed in my boat.

Now, this is not to say that my daughter completely abandoned me. She is too considerate for that.

Whenever there was a slow dance or a novelty song, or she needed her shoe adjusted, or wanted some food or drink, I was her man. And I guess, for the time being that will have to suffice.

But in between the DJ's strategic placement of "Daddy's Little Girl," "Butterfly Kisses," "The Hokey Pokey" and "The Chicken Dance," I pretty much stood by the wayside watching my child grow up before my eyes.

I remembered when she was so tiny I could hold her in one hand. Now I nearly get a hernia every time I try to carry her to bed.

She was dressed like a young woman and yet I couldn't get past memories of a baby's wispy curls.

A toddler in love with water, splashing madly in and out of and through her wading pool.

A five-year-old mastering the secrets of two-wheeled bicycling on the first try. Dashing my plans to spend all day running up and down the street, but filling me with pride in her accomplishment.

And now, she was screaming over Aaron Carter, a boy band member's younger brother who is smart enough to tap into the under-12 crowd with bubble gum music so sweet it gives me a Krispy Kreme sugar buzz just listening to it.

Of course, my argument that Aaron is ripping off of dozens of artists before him, can't sing and will fade like the leaves in autumn when his voice changes, mean nothing to Emma. All she knows is that he's "cute."

And as she and her cronies ran around the dance floor holding hands, giggling and sharing secrets about Lord knows what, I wondered, "What does she mean by 'cute'?"

But I knew that, no matter her definition, she had started down the path toward dates and Friday nights, trips to the mall and makeup.

And away from me.

Seeing the future -- theirs and mine -- I want to know my daughters will find someone who will respect and appreciate them as much as they deserve, and as I try to.

But it's impossible. No one can love and care for and protect them like I can. Still, I know I can't hold their hands forever. And it kills me.

I want to show them around life's dance floor. But nature is starting to cut in.

Praying For Our Teachers – But Not In Our Schools

I like the feeling of prayer.

It's a feeling I wish everyone could have, most especially my kids. But I recognize that there are limits to the power of prayer. Or, at least, to the places where the power should be felt.

The public schools should not be one of those places.

I love the sense of connection between my inner self and our outer God. I like the paradoxical feeling of simultaneous control over my life and reliance on a higher power. I like the quiet escape from all the clattering chaos of the rest of my life.

I pray as the feeling takes me, overwhelms me, moves, me, regardless of its direction or destination. In the middle of a gloriously open forest or surrounded by the plaster and paint of my slightly undersized suburban bedroom.

I pray with others. In church, before meals, at Bible

study. In thanksgiving and celebration, in sorrow and consolation.

As a Christian and a father it is my duty to teach my children to pray for all these reasons, but also for more. In a world filled with disorder, disjointedness and disgust, prayer is one of the few gifts that I can give my children that will retain its value.

Long after we stop kneeling at their bedside, holding hands and thanking God for all the things that ring the bells of their hearts – "Thank you for my purple ball and my new big girl bike," my 4-year-old daughter recently said -- prayer will give my children balance. It will center and anchor their spirits against life's many hard winds.

I want everyone, especially my kids to feel as comfortable with prayer as I do. Yet, I don't want anyone else telling my kids what, how or when to pray. That especially includes their public school teachers.

I am a staunch supporter of and advocate for both public schools and teachers. But I strongly oppose prayer in public schools – including the politically expedient but ultimately silly idea of posting of the 10 Commandments in public school classrooms.

I stand on the usual Constitutional grounds, certainly. It is inherently unfair to use tax dollars – mine or theirs – to impose religious beliefs – mine or theirs -- on children who have no control over the matter or no one to speak for them.

But just as important, it is inherently unfair to shove yet another parental responsibility onto teachers' already-overflowing plates.

Teachers have enough to do trying to ensure

our children can read, write and compute in the 21st century.

Already we ask – demand – teachers to do everything we should but can't or won't. They are to educate our kids, care for their emotional needs and help them grow academically and personally. They do all this and more, then get crucified for doing it. Teachers hardly need to also be responsible for our children's' spiritual growth, too.

No, leading our kids to God is Mom and Dad's job, not Mr. or Ms. Smith's.

I'll gladly keep my responsibility for my kids' religion if teachers will keep their jobs teaching them algebra. Society would be much better off if we just let teachers teach, and parents parent.

I'll say a prayer for all of us.

The Times, They Will Change Only If We Change Them

Pardon me one minute…

I need to quickly check the calendar.

Hmmm…yep, just as I thought.

This is indeed 2004.

But you wouldn't know it…

Because a close friend's recent story would suggest that we're still living in the 1950s, or worse.

And irony of ironies, this story, about overt racism and separatist rhetoric wishing and encouraging people who look and sound differently than the protagonist to go "back to where they came from" comes during the week we mark the 50th anniversary of Brown Vs. the Board of Education.

That landmark 1954 United States Supreme Court decision, you may recall, outlawed the idea that "separate" schools were in any way "equal" or Constitutional.

Yet, 50 years later, my friend's story makes clear that some people still think that anyone who speaks with an accent or whose skin is darker than theirs doesn't deserve the same legal protections or considerations as everyone else.

Here's the tale as I received it:

While serving Will County jury duty and suffering the interminable wait to be called upon (an anguish that only those who have served jury duty can understand) my friend started talking to those around her.

Full disclosure/warning: my friend and her husband are a racially mixed couple. So she is often very emotional about race and racism. But I respect and admire her very much for her passion, which I share.

Anyway, the courthouse conversation centered on "laughing about silly stuff and complaining about how there had to be a better way to call a jury," my friend recounted.

She continued: "One of my fellow prospective jurors suggested that we outsource the jury selection process to India since they were always willing to take the work we didn't want to do…I went back to reading my book."

Now, that's certainly a political statement.

But it's also an accurate comment on our current economic condition -- not something I'd necessarily consider overtly racist, but I could certainly understand my friend's discomfort.

The next day, she overheard talk among another group of women who had formed their own chat group.

One of them told the group how, soon after 9-11, she had been in a grocery store and overheard an Arab (she pronounced it with a long A – as in "A-rab") talking on the phone in his own language.

The woman told the group how she went right

up to him and told him to speak English! "Her three conversation group members nodded their heads in solemn agreement and said if you want to live here you have to speak English or they should all go back where they came from," my friend said.

"I didn't say a word, just moved my seat so I didn't have to listen to such foolishness."

But the capper came at a lunchtime prayer vigil on May 6 – the National Day of Prayer. Figuring it was a good way to spend 90 minutes, my friend sat, watched and listened. A children's group performed a nice dance number. Then the Pledge of Allegiance and National Anthem.

Then a local pastor delivered an invocation in which he made it clear that "we weren't there to praise Buddha or Mohammed, we were there to praise Jesus," my friend said. That comment, of course, triggered a slavish Pavlovian round of applause.

"I sure would hate to be a person of color on trial (in Will County) an have the people I saw in that (jury) room or on the pavilion in front of the courthouse selected as a jury of 'my peers,'" my friend said.

Indeed.

Which brings me back to the calendar.

Calendars are a tool to measure time.

It is time, folks.

Time to move beyond silly, ignorant racism.

Time to recognize that "equality" applies to everyone regardless of who they are, where they come from or what they look or sound like.

This idea is nothing less than the philosophical and

ideological bedrock of our Constitution which – speaking of time – was ratified in 1788.

But, recognizing that calendars don't measure or impact the way people think – that process changes much more glacially, – our country has made various changes to try to improve things as our frail human minds have improved.

In 1954, the highest court in the land officially said enough is enough. In terms of our schools, the United States Supreme Court said equal is equal is equal.

That concept too applies to our courthouses, our communities, and our faith systems.

At some point, ignorance is no longer tolerable. Fifty years seems long enough for that message to sink in and take root, don't you think?

With time, maturity is supposed to take over, remove the blinders of stupidity, and open our eyes and hearts and minds to the bigger picture, which is simply this: that everyone is essentially the same and deserves equal treatment.

That is the most basic guarantee that this great country has held out and continues to promise for all of its generations.

The kind of racism that my friend witnessed in the very place that is supposed to practice and apply and ensure equality in our community is the worst kind of such ignorance.

The time has come – indeed, it came long ago -- to consciously, deliberately oppose hatred and the racism it generates.

As individuals, as families, as a community, we must respect each other, and say it is no longer acceptable.

Adulthood in Only 20 Short, Easy Years!

It was one of those "You've got to be kidding me" moments.

As I headed toward the door, the girls waiting outside for me to cart them to their grandparents' house for the weekend, the phone rang.

I stepped toward it. Then stopped. Torn between the instinct to answer and the urgency in the girls' voices, I delayed an antsy second before picking up.

The Caller ID said "Lewis University." The fine liberal arts school is my alma mater. Home of some of my most wonderful memories and challenging experiences. (Those are not necessarily mutually exclusive, by the by, for you 20 and 30-somethings who think all of life is and always should be a silver-plattered gift.)

"Mr. Tom Hernandez?" asked a female voice.

"This is he." Was this another solicitation for a donation or to buy an alumni registry? Not a good time for that. Plus the girls were waiting for their weekend of grandparent-induced frivolity and freedom. Still, I tried to not be too obvious about my impatience.

"Mr. Hernandez, this is (her name did not stick in my head) with Lewis University."

"Yes, I know that," I thought, inching toward the door, phone in hand, mind already on the errands I'd run after dropping off the kids.

On went the sweet voice – a student, I guessed, a young woman not much older than my own, probably working in the alumni office to save a few dollars of tuition. I did the same thing, earning a stipend as my professor's assistant for a semester.

"We're calling tonight to remind you that this year is the 20th anniversary of your graduation from Lewis and to ask you about your impressions and memories of your time here."

Slam! A hammer hit me square between the eyes.

Synchronistic denial crackled through my brain. Then I quickly did the math.

April 2008…May 1988…Sure enough, 20 years.

Now, a high school anniversary is one thing. Leaving childhood is certainly an important milestone.

Leaving college, though, meant entering adulthood.

It didn't seem like it at the time, but college was for me (and for most people, is) the last clinging grasp to freedom – not from responsibility, certainly. Most college students work very hard and are responsible, more or less, for the cost of their time in school.

Rather, it is a time of freedom from significance.

College is a time to learn about significance. But that significance becomes real only after the diploma is framed and hung on a wall. A token of a road traveled, glanced in passing if at all, as you occupy your station in the adult world.

In this world, everything you do means something to someone other than yourself (or your parents, if you were lucky enough to have mom and dad pay for school.)

Yet, none of this is to diminish the importance of what college gives most students. Certainly, what it gave me.

College is a time for intellectual exploration, experimentation, and expansion. For thinking about and coming to understand who and what and why and how and when. Not just about scholarly subjects and classical issues, but (and more importantly) about yourself.

College grants the luxury, the bittersweet pleasure of leisurely learning. A gift that workingmarriagebabies-billshomerepairsmusiclessonsetcetera doesn't much care for, and usually doesn't give or indulge.

Interestingly, I found myself back at Lewis the next day, rehearsing for the play in which I would soon perform.

Waiting for my turn on stage during a rehearsal, surrounded by college kids with more zip and zeal than I can muster in a week of weeknights, I chatted with an old friend about, of all things, philosophy, faith and religion.

Philosophy, faith and religion were the three subjects I most enjoyed studying at Lewis – my "holy trinity" of learning, as it were. Not surprising, since it's a liberal arts university run by the Christian Brothers.

There I was, wondering and debating (again) about significance and meaning, value and purpose, life's spiritual engine versus its institutional operations.

This is what we in the "belief" business call Godincidence. Nothing happens randomly. Everything is connected. There is meaning everywhere. We just have to be small and quiet enough to seek and see it.

This was my exact life 20 years ago. Talking, a lot, to people of a like mind about things that, perhaps, wouldn't mean a whole lot in the bigger world. But they meant a whole lot in that time, in that place.

They meant a whole lot to the person I was. And to the one I would become, 20 years later.

From the Mouths of Babes, Wisdom Comes

I have been de-Grinched.

Remember how, in the holiday classic "How the Grinch Stole Christmas" the Grinch learned that Christmas wasn't about materialism but rather love?

He thought that if he removed all the holiday stuff from every house in Who-Ville he'd keep Christmas from coming. So he took everything he could lay his green, furry hands on -- toys, ornaments, food, even the tacks that held the decorations on the walls.

Yet on Christmas morning, the Who's celebrated anyway.

Disregarding their gift-less state, they clasped hands and sang one of the most beautiful Christmas songs ever written. The response to his night of thievery was so unexpected that the Grinch's heart grew two sizes right there on the spot.

Lately, I confess, I had become something of a Grinch about Christmas. Naturally cynical and professionally skeptical, I came to believe that every child saw Christmas as little more than one big trip to the toy store. Modern parenthood will do that.

For months my wife and I have endured our girls shouting "Mommy, Daddy I want that!" with every strategically placed commercial during Nickelodeon's daily fare of kid's programming. It got so bad that we didn't even bother to turn to the television to see the object of their (very brief and transient) desire. We'd just nod our heads and dully chant, "Yes, we know."

Yet, recently, it was also a group of Plainfield children who showed me the presumptuous error of my ways. Not every person -- and certainly not every child – thinks of Christmas in material terms.

Wanting to provide a springboard on my church's radio show for a conversation about "the real meaning of Christmas," I asked about 20 kids of various ages at our church what Christmas means to them.

There were the predictable responses, especially from the very youngest: gifts, Santa Claus, gifts, decorations, Rudolph the Red-Nosed Reindeer, gifts, Frosty the Snowman, more gifts.

But strikingly, most of the kids, from the first-grade class on up focused instead on the holiday's religious background.

Their words, filled with real warmth of understanding melted away the ice around my own heart.

Christmas is a day to celebrate Jesus' birth, they said; to spend time with family and friends; to share our joy with others; to remember and help people who aren't as lucky as us; finally and ultimately to love, as Jesus would grow up to do, and did, and does.

Sure, we Grinches might say, these were church-ed kids, speaking in church. What else would they say?

But that's the point. Kids say just what they want and mean. It's we adults who analyze the situation before responding, shaping our answers to fit the context of the questions. "He's asking this, so he must want to hear that," we think, mentally mapping our path, and congratulating ourselves for our supposed cunning.

Not these kids. They knew. What's more, they were brave enough, among peers, to say so.

Certainly Christmas isn't just about toys and decorations and lights and parties and stuff. These things are just trappings – bows and glitter and colorful paper -- that have grown out of our experience of the event of Jesus' birth.

In the same way, Christmas isn't really even about Jesus' birth, per se. The Christian church didn't start officially celebrating Christmas until the fourth century, and only then largely as a counter to the pagan winter solstice celebrations, according to Biblical scholarship.

Most of the details we now associate with Christmas – the virgin birth, the manger scene, the Magi, the guiding star, the shepherds, Joseph and Mary's return to Bethlehem – come to us from mythical birth narratives written decades after Jesus' death, by gospel writers making specific theological points.

Yet, all of it, from the Biblical stories to modern Western capitalism speaks to the simple, direct spiritual connection with God that Jesus taught and personified – the love, community and forgiveness.

Lots of adults get too wrapped up in the details. We overthink, overanalyze and outsmart ourselves. We tie ourselves into emotional, spiritual and psychological knots. And then we vainly wonder why our lives seem so empty.

Then as now, leave it to the children to feel the spirit. To understand the wisdom. To speak the truth.

Hello? I'll Call You Right Back

Rudeness is rising to new heights.

Like, the heights of a satellite. The ones that bounce cell phone calls into every corner of the world – including the ones with unsuspecting and uninterested ears.

I don't mean the two people on either end of the actual conversation. I mean the rest of us unfortunates who have to suffer the personal back-and-forth of those who use cell phones in public places.

When it seemed like people couldn't be any more inconsiderate, the so-called "information age" gave us one more way to be thoughtless about those around us: cell phones.

Recently I wrote about the ubiquity of cell phones in our culture (for those unwilling to put your phone down long enough to look up "ubiquity," it means that they're everywhere).

It seemed I had stumbled onto the one person in the free world who didn't have one. And I wondered, satirically, how she got along without one attached to her hip.

You know how, when you're looking to buy a car, you notice every other car passing by?

Since writing that original column, I've noticed every yahoo within 50 miles talking on their cell phones. Everywhere. All the time. Incessantly. Without any consideration for anyone else's personal space or privacy.

Sadly, this is yet another example of the breakdown of good behavior. The creaking collapse of culture. The miasmatic rise of bad manners.

Newsflash to everyone under 30 years old:

I don't want to see every guy's underwear rising above his pants.

I don't want to see every girl's bra straps.

I don't want to hear every man, woman and child – yes, child -- dropping the F-bomb in casual, public conversation like a gourmet peppering a salad.

And I don't want to hear your cell phone conversations while I wait in line at the Burger King. Or at the gas station. Or in the movie theater. Or at the baseball game.

Or. Anywhere. Else.

Those are your conversations. Have them. But keep them to yourself.

Because, when you so thoughtlessly share them in public, what you're really doing is infringing on my rights.

My right to my personal space -- if I wanted the latest update on the party you just came from or are going to, I'd invite you to dinner.

My right to quick and speedy service – as the clerk

asks you for the fifth time "What did you say?" as you continue to babble into your phone at the counter, slowing down and inconveniencing everyone behind you.

My right to feel reasonably safe and secure -- every time you enter a public place talking on a cell phone, weaving unfocused through the aisles and then exiting with phone still to your ear, words flying 16 to a beat, I quickly pray that you're going to stop talking before you get behind the wheel of your car.

To be fair, it's not just consumers who have become inconsiderate cell phone jerks.

My wife recently tried to buy sandwiches at a local Subway restaurant. She went to pay for our food – that is to say, to give over some of our hard-earned money which helps pay employees' salaries.

Money which could have been spent at any of a dozen other places offering the same basic menu. Money which we pay in trade for the reasonable expectation of decent service.

The clerk never, not once, ever put down her cell phone as she assembled three sandwiches and completed the order. The call, based on what my wife could hear, was personal.

My wife shared this story with me. I insisted that she call the manager. "The manager needs to know about this," I huffed. She said – and here's the kicker – "I think (the clerk) was the manager."

Clearly, this is not new. Clerks forever have been known to continue talking to coworkers as they wait on customers. But cell phones have raised the bar on ignominious ignorance.

I realize I may be waging a one man war.

I know the world has changed.

I know I am closing in on death by the day.

But there is still a place in this world for common courtesy. There is still a need for decorum. There is still value in self control and, yes Lord, a little modesty.

How does the old saying go? "Guns don't kill people. People kill people?"

Well, cell phones don't make people rude. Rude people use cell phones. All the time. Anywhere.

Dinosaurs, Space Aliens, and People Without Cell Phones

I cannot believe one actually exists!

Something so rare that it strains the imagination. Expands reality. Stretches the bounds of credulity.

No, not a dinosaur. They're a dime a dozen – at least their skeletons are – pieced together and propped in the entryways of every decent museum around the world.

Not a spaceship. You don't have to wear an aluminum foil suit to believe, if only just a little bit, that they could possibly be real. And besides, pictures (real or fake, you decide) of UFOs have existed for years.

Not conservatives who plan to vote Democratic this fall. Reagan Democrats already broke this ground back in the 1980s. It's perfectly reasonable for a "party lifer" to like an opposing party candidate's personality enough to vote the other way once or twice.

No, more bizarre and shocking than all of these, I talked to someone recently who does not – let me repeat that in case you missed it – <u>does not</u> have or use a cell phone!

Who in the world in 2008 doesn't have a cell phone? Who doesn't rely on the ubiquitous device for every means and manner of communications? Some sort of social weirdo? A cultural freak? A time warp tragedy?

Nope. Just a mom. A regular, every day person who said she doesn't need a cell phone.

Actually, she had one for some time, but recently gave it up. And, lo and behold, her world has not collapsed! Her universe has not started to unravel. Her reality has not begun to crumble.

That these thoughts crossed my mind is a strange testament to the power of the cell phone, which has been commercially available for only a relative-few years.

Much like the desktop computer and, later, the Internet, the cell phone has taken over the world so quickly that it's hard to remember a time without them.

But it wasn't that long ago. One of my favorite movies is "Running Scared", made in 1986. Billy Crystal and Gregory Hines played Chicago cops chasing down a drug dealer played by Jimmy Smits. A very underrated movie.

In one of the funniest scenes, the detectives steal Smits' car to flush him out of hiding. While in the car, they use Smits' then-revolutionary car phone to call him.

The car phone – the grandparent to today's cell phone – was as big as a brick. It was right out of a WWII movie, but was considered the sharpest part of technology's cutting edge in the middle 1980s. I mean, the drug dealer had it, not the cops. So it had to be cool.

Anyone seeing that movie today – especially anyone born after 1986 – cannot help but laugh when they see the phone.

Today, everyone has some kind of palm-sized cellular

device on their belt, in a purse or hanging out of their ears. Even kids have them for their "safety." Each of our daughters got one when they were 12.

Seventh grade seemed to be the appropriate nexus of maturity, responsibility, social obligation, and necessity. My wife and I both worked during the day when school let out, so the kids were to use the cell phone to check in when they left school.

But really, do we need them?

Do we need to be constantly available? Is anything so important that someone must always be able to reach me RIGHT AT THIS MINUTE?

And none of this gets to the extended cell phone-generated communications quandaries created by text messages, videos, and pictures.

Of course, 99.9 percent of us would say "Yes." The information-driven world we live in demands this level of accessibility.

Or does it? How did we get along before cell phones took over the world?

How did we talk to our kids after school then?

Why, -- gasp! -- we trusted that they would get home safely. And then they'd call us from home. Or – heaven forbid – one of the parents, usually mom, was at home waiting for them.

How did we check messages while out of the office? Gosh, we'd have to call from our destination and talk to a secretary or assistant.

And, how could our bosses reach us in the car or after hours? Well, shock of all shockers, they didn't. Enough said about that one.

It could be said that the PCP (Pre-Cell Phone) world

was less communicative, more simplistic, less efficient. And yet, somehow, the world continued to revolve, the sun still came up, and life went on.

Is this right or wrong? Could we really live without cell phones? Well, I think...Wait, my cell phone just rang.

Hold on, it's my boss. I've got to take this call...

Still Waiting, Happily, for My Lunch

On January 9, 1997, I got cheated out of a free birthday lunch.

Not that I hold grudges…but that memory rolled back over the shores of my brain's beach recently as I observed a memorial service for the father of a dear family friend.

Actually, I kind of participated – though only accidentally – and it was that participation that jostled loose the memory of my lost lunch.

See, my friend's father was a Navy veteran. As part of his memorial service, a trio of sailors performed a flag ceremony and presented the flag to his daughter, who is my wife's best friend.

I saw the same ceremony performed at my own father's funeral. He died on January 9, 1997 at the incredibly-too-early age of 51, after suffering a massive heart attack.

Seeing the flag ceremony again, without warning, raised hot tears in my eyes. I struggled, somewhat unsuccessfully, to choke down my own emotions, not wanting to take anything away from my friend's opportunity to grieve the loss of her dad.

And yet, I left that memorial service, not as upset as one might have expected (though it would have been difficult to watch the beautiful precision and respect of the flag ceremony without welling up in any case).

Rather, I realized that the memorial service was more about my friend's dad's life, than about his death.

Although the last element of the service was sad, everything leading up to it was a celebration of his time on earth. His childhood, young adulthood, parenthood, professional accomplishments, spiritual and church life. Even his last few weeks when he and his family debated the wisdom of maintaining his connection to life support.

People told stories. They laughed. They celebrated. They remembered, with some sadness, but mostly with joy, the life of a man whose person had indelibly marked and shaped their own existence.

Then a new thought occurred -- that this is what our passing should be about. Not about mourning death and dying. They are inevitable and therefore somewhat boring.

Rather, our passing should be a chance to celebrate our life, which is nothing if not unexpected, surprising, shocking, hysterical, funny, maddening, frustrating, exhilarating, irritating, pointless and chock-full with meaning and great exaltation – and often all in the same moment.

Come to think of it, why wait until we die to celebrate life?

Why not try to do it every day? Find a few minutes to

simply reflect on whatever it is that is good in our lives? Remember those who have helped us become whatever it is we have become. And say thanks.

Hey, I'm no Pollyanna. Or "Paulyanna" as the case may be. I know as well as anyone that not everything in life is good. Not every step is taken along a yellow brick road. There will be pain. Sometimes even misery. Often it will seem unbearable.

But even sadness brings something to life – it focuses the lens through which our joy is found and magnified.

On January 9, 1997 I lost my father just as I was learning how to be a young dad. We did not agree on much through my childhood and early adulthood. We were just starting to find and navigate a common ground, to connect and bond, through my infant children, his grandchildren.

Not a day goes by that I don't wish he were still here, that a question doesn't arise, that a thought doesn't occur that I wish I could bounce off of him.

Seeing what my friend's family did to remember her dad reminded me that too much sadness is time wasted.

In that vein, I should clarify that my dad was a great jokester. He would regularly and often make lunch or coffee dates and then never show up. No calls saying he was running late. He just wouldn't go. Everyone understood. It was just my dad.

Reviewing January 9, 1997 now through the filter of my recent experience, it occurs to me that my dad may have died just to get out buying me lunch.

Of course, that's a joke. But it's also my personal celebration.

It could be said, truly and accurately, that my dad's

death was cruelly unfair to me, my brothers, our children, and certainly his wife.

It could be said. But it won't be here. Why bother? Mourning his death won't bring him back to life. Yet celebrating his life will help keep him alive, if only in our hearts.

A Truer Love Story Has Never Been Told...

Before my last name supplanted hers, my wife hated my guts.

Believe it or not, this is a story of true love, though it is both "Post" and "Anti" Valentine's Day. Because just after Valentine's Day in 1985, my life changed.

On February 21, 1985, Kellie became my future. We have spent more than half of our lives together.

That two teens fell in love is neither particularly unique nor especially interesting, until one considers our relationship prior to that first date.

She absolutely despised me.

Kellie and I met our senior year in high school. We were both new to the school, and so didn't know each other.

As she described me, I was a pompous egomaniac bent on controlling the school, if not the world. In hindsight, she was more right than wrong. Kellie has smoothed my rough edges considerably. But, fully unfurled, I can still be a tough flag to salute.

I certainly had an air of confidence thanks to my involvement in numerous student activities. And I was rightly proud of my several positions of student leadership. But all Kellie saw was overbearing hubris.

We didn't "meet cute."

In fact our first encounters only strengthened her perception of me. I was editor of the student newspaper; she typed copy on the then-new computer system. (Yes, though my children refuse to believe it, we are old enough to remember when there were no computers...)

Kellie also had the added pleasure of watching me fawn daily over my girlfriend du jour.

As most teenagers do at some point in most of their young relationships, I seriously thought I would spend the rest of my life with this young woman.

"The rest of my life" lasted about five months.

Fast forward to the December of my freshman year in college. My faith in women had only recently been restored, but was still fragile, after the aforementioned girlfriend had ripped my heart from its moorings, stomped on and handed back to me the prior spring.

But the lovelorn and common sense are often strangers.

The ex-girlfriend asked me for a ride to a holiday party at a mutual friend's house. I obliged, thinking that this was her way of re-stoking our past embers. The only fire was in my heart. The only smoke, in my eyes.

The ex-girlfriend merely needed a ride and, to make matters worse, she met another guy at the party.

Luckily for me, Kellie also came to the shindig. Trying to make my ex jealous, I sidled up to Kellie in the ex's line of sight and planted a holiday smooch on her cheek.

To this day, my wife says that kiss turned everything around. I didn't think it was particularly innovative or memorable, as kisses go. But, what do I know? I've never kissed myself.

Ever the dense man (I understand from many women that that phrase is redundant) I missed her flashing-neon signals of interest for two months.

But we finally went on our first date, a college dance, on February 20, 1985. The next day, I called the three other girls I was haphazardly dating and wished them all a happy life.

Many years later, I am still cynical, sarcastic and doubting. My tongue is only partly in cheek when I say that people are like stray cats. If you keep feeding them, they'll keep coming around. I don't like cats, and I tend not to trust most people, at least at first.

But, among countless life lessons my wife has taught me, I have learned from Kellie that most people are very nice if only given a chance. (Cats still irritate me, though.)

Kellie has an amazing vision of the heart, a quality I lack, admire and covet. She saw through my flinty veneer.

But, more than merely being able to see through me, she wanted to see through me. And when I fought her peeking into my soul, she smiled and laughed until I let my guard down.

All these years later, she still laughs at me. Most of the time it is with love in her heart. The other times? Well, let's just say I often reap what I sow. But I am glad to have her by my side as we plow through life together.

Just don't tell anyone I said so. I don't want people to think I'm a nice guy.

This Is What God Meant When He First Said "Blue"

Skipping a stone well is a science.

I know. I've been skipping stones my whole life – and I'm pretty good at it. I'm proud to say that, armed with the right stone, multiple and high-flying skips are often the norm.

I brag, because skipping stones is one of my few real abilities – not to be confused with talent, which I believe is God-given. Ability, however, can be learned and taught.

The stone has to be flat, but not too flat. It must have some heft, but cannot weigh too much. It must be spun out of the hand perfectly parallel to the water, which should be as calm as possible. The errant wave, no matter how small, can ruin an otherwise-excellent throw.

The idea is to transfer enough energy from the hand to the energy-less rock so that when its flat surface hits the water's flat surface, the inevitable friction is heightened enough to send the stone jumping, flying and pirouetting in mid-air.

Two, three, four, five, yes, even six times, before finally melding with its watery grave, another thousand years away from conquering the beachhead again.

Many hours were spent and scores of stones thrown explaining and demonstrating these physics to my youngest daughter as we vacationed recently in Copper Harbor, the furthest north outpost in Michigan's Upper Peninsula.

My family camps.

Mom and dad, kids, maternal grandparents and sister-in-law, all together.

We always have a great time.

That, in itself, is something of an achievement, as my mother-in-law points out: not many families can spend more than a few hours together even under the best conditions, much less for 10 days in the great out of doors where one cannot hide behind the distraction of holiday festivities to avoid family politics.

In a tent, there's little room for bad attitudes.

But this year's outing was the cream of the recent crop.

This part of Michigan, on Lake Superior, is breathtakingly beautiful.

Woods as deep and lush as anything the Northwest can offer, framed by skies so blue that this is what God must have meant when the word "blue" first passed His lips.

Long and numerous biking and walking trails. Hundreds of thousands of rocks to sift through in the hunt for just the right rock – or as it turned out, a bucket-full of them – to bring home.

Just enough civilization – just far enough down the

road – to ensure that no one will have to impersonate the Donner gang to survive, but won't be kept up at night by traffic speeding down the highway 200 feet from your sleeping bag.

But, corny as it sounds, the best part of our family vacation is time spent with the family.

We ate most of our meals together outdoors, where certain foods – hotdogs, hamburgers in particular –taste better than they ever have inside a restaurant.

My poor father-in-law, a grandchild's dream, ate more marshmallows around the nightly campfire than any human should have to endure – burned to a charcoal-y crisp by my oldest child, because "That's how Grampa likes them," she insisted.

And we talked. About everything. Presidential politics. Education. Overpaid sports stars. Work. Rest. Music. The numerous reports of bears entering the campground. Other campers, especially those who left out coolers and food products, attracting bears into the campground.

We laughed hard at family stories told many times before, yet still funny -- no longer for their newness, but rather for the exuberance and joy of their telling, especially by my sister-in-law, a natural born storyteller if ever there was one.

We all know the punch lines. We all know what's coming. But that knowledge binds us.

Now, to some, perhaps many, these may seem like very simple things to commemorate. Green trees? Skipping rocks? Eating together? Telling jokes?

I agree.

These are very simple pleasures. Exceptionally easy to manufacture and share.

So then, why don't we do more of it?

In a world where progress is often measured by the ever-increasing complexity of the system polluting our minds, sapping our bodies and corrupting our spirits, we need the simplicity of spending real time, doing simple things, together.

Skipping a stone or two is a good place to start.

"UnkTom, What Dat?"

I should have seen it coming.

I should have noticed the pattern – the rapid-fire accumulation of seemingly-simple questions. But my nephew is so darned cute that I was temporarily drawn off guard.

"UnkTom" – each query, and there seemed to be hundreds that day, began with this – "What dat?"

His chubby finger pointed innocently, to a bag of dry mustard on my chef-wife's work table. "Mustard," I said.

"UnkTom, what dat?"

Another bag of spice. "Pepper."

"UnkTom, what dat?"

A second variety of pepper, I explained.

"UnkTom, what dat?"

"Garlic."

And then, the walls came tumbling down.

He paused for a second, drawing adequate breath to perform his coup de grace.

Pointing to a plastic baggie holding about 50 packets

of vegetable and flower seeds, he looked at me, a sweet smile disguising his malevolent plan. He was subtle and clean, like a stiletto-wielding professional assassin. I know he's only 3, but I swear he knew just what he was doing.

"UnkTom, whatdat?"

"Seeds," I said, thinking that my umbrella answer would suffice. Such arrogance fathers many a fool.

Alex began pointing to every packet, repeating the same inquiry for each. Finally, after identifying about a dozen packets, teetering dangerously between exhaustion and exasperation, I shouted, "They're all seeds!"

But he wasn't quite finished.

He looked at me, square in the eyes, and hit me with one more verbal volley:

"UnkTom?"

"What?"

"UnkTom, why?"

I felt like I was in a Salvadore Dali painting, my head melting into my hands.

I mentally retreated. Reminded myself that Alex is a toddler. Toddlers are naturally, boundlessly inquisitive. Like dogs, they don't understand finite concepts like time, space, or Uncle Tom's patience.

Remember too, I thought, that this task of keeping Alex occupied was fair trade for my brother, his dad, helping me put in a new bathroom floor. A chore I had been strategically avoiding since I tore up a chunk of tile two years ago to check for a leak.

My wife finally insisted that it be fixed. She bribed me with breakfast, then dragged me to Menards to buy new tile.

The next thing I knew, my brother called me at work

to "offer" to help with any home chores I might have to do. A mere coincidence, he insisted. Indeed...

The only thing was, he'd have to bring his son, since my sister-in-law also had to work.

Now, I love Alex, as I love all of my nieces and nephews. But he's a breed apart. Alex is a nice mixture of his parents, physically.

Yet when it comes to personality, he is an exact replica of his dad -- an evil genius.

Exceptionally bright, curious, funny, naturally talented, creative, clever, often to the point of hair-pulling vexation.

My brother Paul (and probably his son, down the line) is like the stock comic book character – think Lex Luthor – who could use his brilliant mind for good or evil, but chooses evil because it's more fun.

Of course, Paul hasn't done anything evil. But I do believe he is a genius. His intellect is sharp as a thousand Ginsu knives. Give him time...

To fill the time, Alex and I went for a walk. We watched "Scooby Doo" cartoons until I remembered why I stopped watching them as a kid -- they all end the same way.

We cleaned up the dog poop in the back yard – well, I cleaned and Alex chased his balloons around the yard until they popped against the rose bushes. We played with our Shi-Tzu, Ozzie, with whom Alex is fascinated, because he's the smallest dog he's seen.

All the while, Alex continued his personal "Spanish Inquisition" of me, asking about everything in his seemingly-limitless view.

Finally, he fell asleep.

I muttered a quick, sincere prayer of thanks. Then I insisted that my brother let me help with my own project. He insisted harder that I was doing more than my share by taking care of Alex.

Sibling sympathy? Prideful workmanship? Control-freakish domination? Who knows? Who cares? I was worn out. Bushed. Beat.

Anyway, we spent two whole weekend days at this. Paul putting in my floor, not letting me do anything, insisting that it was more helpful for me to watch Alex.

In the end, we had a great time. We talked, joked, laughed, shared lunch and dinner with our families. And I connected more with my nephew. Beyond merely laying tile, we were building family.

Meanwhile, my brother did a terrific job with the floor. And he has already made plans to remodel the rest of my bathroom, despite my lack of interest, funding or ability to assist. But he was adamant -- he'd do it, and even pay for it.

I am pretty sure that what he really wants is another break from Daddy-duty. He is my brother. So I will be happy to oblige. Plus, I'll get a new bathroom out of the deal.

If I survive Alex, that is.

Here, Bunny, Bunny, Bunny

"Did you kill them?"

I heard the strange and frightening inquiry from two distinctly different people.

"No!" I said, shocked at the blunt, direct, cold, compassionless note of the question.

They may have been unconnected individuals. But they shared one thought.

"You should kill them. They'll just destroy your garden."

I know, I know, I confessed. But how do you kill something that is so cute?

As any parent knows and will attest, under different circumstances I could easily be talking about my children. But, fortunately, this time the conversation was around six baby bunnies (or unfortunately, if you're a baby bunny.)

A few weeks ago, after a long afternoon of yard work, I noticed what looked like a patch of dead grass and dry dirt in my yard, about 10 feet in from the fence.

I toed at it absentmindedly, trying to figure out if I

had accidentally sprayed week killer here, and if so, how did I spray so far into the yard.

The dirt moved under my shoe, loosely, as if someone had dug a hole and haphazardly covered it up. Now I wondered if one of the kids had, for some reason, buried something here.

Weird thought, I know, especially since I have teens. Their days of hiding "treasure" in the sand box are long gone – as is the sand box. Still, that's what was running through my mind, when suddenly, the whole patch broke loose.

It was dusk. So I couldn't be sure of what I saw…but it looked like…yes, it seemed that…sure enough…

"Holy sh--!" I yelled. My wife turned her head toward my exclamation.

"Something is moving in here!"

Hidden under the dirt were six pink, hairless, wrinkled little…well, I didn't know what they were at first. My wife looked at them.

"Are they mice?" she asked. "No, I think they're bunnies," she said, ignoring my non-response, talking more to herself than to me. "This is a rabbit hutch."

A rabbit hutch?

Hutches are no surprise to the common gardener. And my garden skills are nothing if not common, so I've seen many a hutch before --shallow depressions and small holes dug under one of the many ground cover plants along our fence line.

But I'd never seen or imagined one being in the yard itself, smack dab out in the open. And when I say "in the open," I mean it. My wife fancies birds. She has turned our back yard into an aviary, with about a dozen feeders scattered around and under and throughout the trees.

All of those finches and cardinals and woodpeckers and red winged blackbirds and grackles and morning doves make for a cacophonous and beautiful scene.

They also make for a great smorgasbord for the neighborhood hawks, which routinely start hovering around our neck of the woods every few weeks.

What if a hawk swooped down and had a bunny-snack?

Figuring we can't do much to stop nature, we covered the bunnies back up. My wife marked the area with garden sticks so that I wouldn't accidentally run over them with the lawnmower.

I did some quick research on the Internet. Sure enough, bunnies are born live, hairless, deaf and blind. The mother covers them up, then returns to the hutch once a day, for only a few minutes, to feed them.

Over the next week or so, we watched that precise process play out. We never saw the momma. But each day we saw the bunnies get bigger, grow fur, and eventually get too big for their makeshift home.

One morning all we found was an empty dirt patch between the gardening sticks. Our babies – er, I mean, the bunnies – were gone.

My wife shared this Mother Nature Moment with her mother, a gifted master gardener. She is also a wonderful, kind, caring mother and grandmother extraordinaire.

She was the first to ask why we didn't kill the rabbits.

They're a nuisance, she said. They'll eat your plants and vegetables (many of which she gave us in the first place years ago. Hence, she had some personal interest in the matter.)

Of course I knew this.

I have spent many hours over several summers erecting what I thought were impenetrable chicken wire fences to keep the rabbits out of our vegetable beds.

I have applied gallons of a horrible smelling spray that is supposed to keep rabbits away, but ends up only making me reek of putrescent eggs and garlic.

But they always seem to find a way in.

Then, my buddy Chuck, another self-proclaimed naturalist and gardening enthusiast, said the same thing. Except, Chuck being a former newspaper man like myself, used words that cannot be printed here to describe the furry little intruders.

Admittedly, they are both right.

The bunnies will eat our plants. They will nibble our lettuce. They will, despite our best efforts, find more secret entrances into our yard than David Copperfield uses in his stage show. And, even when we think we've gotten rid of them, they'll make more little bunnies.

We shouldn't welcome them. I should have drowned them in their hutch, as Chuck suggested.

But they're so darned cute…

Red AND White AND Blue

This is the stuff that really torques me.

A recent story ran all over the media about Plainfield resident Debra Brzostowski flying an American flag upside down outside her house to protest the sad state of the economy.

According to published reports, the U.S. Flag Code says "the flag should never be displayed with the union down, except as a signal of dire distress in instances of extreme danger to life or property."

Brzostowski said she's feeling plenty distressed by the economy, which has already caused her husband to close his small business. She's having a tough time of it too with her own small telecommunications business.

The couple hasn't made a mortgage payment since June, according to published reports. She's reached out for help from investors and banks. But no one has reached back.

She said she e-mailed local and national government officials including the current and next presidents.

When she got no response from anyone she did what every American has the right to do – she protested her government. She spoke out. Quietly, in a way that harms no one.

Yet, some people have criticized her for turning the flag upside down. They claim doing so is "unpatriotic."

Now, "unpatriotic" is an interesting word in America. For those new to the concept of free speech, ours is one of the few countries in human history that actually allows, protects and even, to a degree encourages its people to protest their government.

And this is where my own sense of patriotism gets twisted like a flag around a pole, shredded by gale force winds of jingoistic ignorance.

The American ideal is not black OR white. Or, more to the point, red OR white OR blue. Rather, it is black AND white, red AND white AND blue.

The system that our forefathers created is not simple or simplistic. It is complex, convoluted, self-contradicting. It shouldn't work. Yet, somehow, it has, and does. And the string holding it all together is our freedom of expression. Difference of opinion is, you know, a good thing in America.

More dangerous than anything Brzostowski has done are the small minds of all persuasions that insist that America is, and can only be, "this or that."

Debra Brzostowski shouldn't be criticized. She should be celebrated.

She should be raised up on solid American shoulders amid thousands of cheering fans. She should get a tickertape parade. Except that the stock market is in such bad shape that Wall Street probably can't afford to throw away the tickertape anymore.

Flying the flag upside down to protest the economy is unpatriotic and disrespectful? Really? To whom?

The military? Hardly.

Soldiers are sworn to uphold and defend the ideals that the flag represents. Those include, most especially, freedom of speech, and the right to protest ones government, so long as it's done peaceably.

Much more disrespectful is to send hundreds of thousands of young men and women to fight a war that made little sense when it started, and makes even less sense now. To try to build a justification for the deaths of more than 4,000 American fighting men and women on the ever-shifting sands of a nonsensical personal/political vendetta.

No, flying a flag upside down as a protest is neither unpatriotic nor disrespectful. In fact, it's not even that clever.

A quick Internet search turned up many examples of many people flying the flag upside down for many reasons.

As expected, some – including a military veteran -- have done so to protest the Iraq war.

Ironically, in 2007 one person flew the flag upside down to protest the government's plan to withdraw troops from Iraq.

On the silver screen, soldiers flew the flag upside down to alert military commanders to corruption and abuses in a military prison in "The Last Castle," a 2001 movie with Robert Redford and James Gandolfini.

Flags have flown upside down even in the world of politics.

In 1999, that ultra right-wing nut ball and political carpetbagger Alan Keyes wore his flag lapel pin upside down and encouraged "American patriots wear and exhibit our nation's flag turned upside-down as a symbol of the nation's distress" to protest President's Clinton's impeachment acquittal.

Indeed, the United States Supreme Court in 1989 said flag burning is a protected form of free speech. I'm no Constitutional scholar, but it would seem that, in light of that ruling turning a flag upside down to protest the government's response to the collapsing economy is in no way unpatriotic.

It's over the top, certainly. Melodramatic. Overstatement. Perhaps even ill-advised insofar as the action is essentially a military code. She could have awoken to unknowing soldiers and tanks to her front lawn in response.

But unpatriotic? Disrespectful? Please.

America has a lot of challenges right now. The last thing it needs is more small-minded, ignorant zealotry. The last eight years have provided a surplus of that.

We need more people like Debra Brzostowski. Americans brave enough to live the American dream – which includes the right to tell the government when it's wrong.

The Problem with Kids Today…

He took little Susie to the junior prom
"Excitable boy," they all said
And he raped her and killed her then he took her home
"Excitable boy," they all said.

The lyrics, from "Excitable Boy", the late, great Warren Zevon's paean to bad parenting, came immediately to mind when I read the story.

Not to mention anger, disgust and a little embarrassment on behalf of all parents everywhere.

A recent story in the Chicago Tribune detailed how some Highland Park parents got mad at a limousine driver because he called the police when their high school-age kids tried to smuggle alcohol onto his "party bus" on homecoming night.

According to the story, one of the teens offered the driver money to "look the other way," told the driver that the paper bag containing alcohol was "none of his business," and, when the driver refused to cooperate with the teens, eventually begged him to not call their parents.

The driver called the cops. The cops arrested 13 teens and charged them with underage drinking.

As bad as all of that is – and it's plenty bad – it's basically stupid, time-honored teenage tradition.

What's worse is that some of the parents actually got mad at the driver and even threatened to sue the owner of the limousine company, according to the newspaper.

Some of the angry parents wrote off the behavior because it was homecoming.

The story continued, saying that while "most agree (the driver) did the right thing, experts say the incident raises questions about the fallout from such vigilance. For example, will teens avoid oversight by adults and drive themselves the next time, even when drunk"

Well sure they will. Because teens are, by nature, not the brightest bulbs in the box. Science confirms this. Recent research shows conclusively that human brains don't fully develop the part that makes long-term decisions until they're in their early 20s.

In other words, most teens are literally incapable of thinking beyond the moment. And if the moment involves danger, booze, sex, drugs, basically any kind of risk, well, so much the better.

But what kind of a parent excuses their child breaking the law – and for an excuse as flimsy, random, arbitrary and just plain stupid as homecoming?

What in the world is going on here? I was so exasperated reading this story that I almost screamed out loud at the newspaper. The only thing worse than teenagers not acting their age, is parents not acting theirs.

You know what is wrong with some kids today? Their parents.

Don't these parents know the damage they're doing to their own kids by excusing their youthful indiscretions, not to mention the potential harm to the rest of the world that their precious darlings could do?

What happens later when, God forbid, the kid does something worse, like seriously hurting someone? Hello, Warren Zevon? I know you're in heaven, but can you sing a little louder?

The newspaper cited another so-called expert saying the incident raises the question of whether the drinking age should be lowered to 18. A valid point deserving serious debate.

But the point, while good, is also moot.

Who cares what the law might be someday? The law today says no drinking alcohol before age 21. Right or wrong, the law is the law is the law.

This limo driver deserves commendation, not criticism from a bunch of adolescents masquerading as mommies and daddies.

Kids will be kids, and teens will try pretty much anything that they think they can get away with. That's how it's always been. That's how it will always be.

What's changed is the number of parents willing to ignore, or worse, defend their kids' bad behavior. If the kids get caught flying too close to the sun, then they should have to fall, and suffer the pain of any resulting bumps and bruises.

The parents should face the same consequences as their underage children. After all, parents are morally, ethically and legally responsible for their progeny until the kids aren't kids anymore.

Lord knows I crossed many lines as a teen and young adult (though not as many as either of my brothers, who were both braver than me when it came to tempting fate.) But I drew the line at some activities and tests because I was more afraid of what my dad might do than any other fallout I might face.

With luck and a lot of hard work, our children will like and appreciate us. But ultimately, friendship and appreciation are secondary concerns to respect. And respect requires just a dash of fear.

A little pain, and then fear of that pain happening again, is how kids learn to not touch a hot stove. The same applies to growing up.

Shame on those Highland Park teens for trying to take advantage of that limo driver.

But double shame on those parents who tried to excuse their kids' bad behavior, and in so doing, ignored their parental responsibilities.

The secret to good parenting is amazingly simple.

Be a parent.

Welcome to Our Torture Chamber

Our house is a deathtrap.

I came recently to that sad realization while watching three of our godchildren, who range in age from 10 years to 1 year old.

Time never passes faster, or more obviously, than when one goes backwards. Babysitting when you are years beyond the "baby" stage is like climbing into a super-nuclear charged time machine and throwing it into "R".

Frankly, as the parents of a teen and a pre-teen who know our expectations, habits and rules, who can and do pretty much entertain themselves, it's very easy to forget what it's like to have young children around.

The 10-year-old and her middle sister, age 6, posed no real challenges except for meeting their finicky eating habits. Our own children tend to not fuss too much about eating, especially breakfast.

My wife, a professional chef, whipped up homemade chocolate chip pancakes for the elder goddaughters. Each plate became a smiley face with garnish of fresh cut strawberries for the hair, bananas for the eyes and nose and orange slices for the mouth.

A kid's living, breathing dream, right? Not for Devon and Claire. They ate the fruit, nibbled at the pancake, and, predictably, claimed to be hungry an hour later.

But it turned out that that was the least of our concerns.

While her older sisters were eating their breakfast, the baby, Aubrey, was eating a dog biscuit. Not by design – at least, not by our design.

The dog, which by this time was hiding behind the couch, unused to so much commotion on a Sunday morning, had strategically hidden his treat in one of his many secret spots.

Somehow, using a toddler's radar-like sixth sense -- more sophisticated than anything the military has devised -- Aubrey found the cookie. She was in full gnaw, laughing and drooling, before either my wife or I could get across the room.

Then, after tiring of a box full of metal and wooden measuring spoons, whisks, bowls, and assorted other amusingly noisy, bang-y, clang-y gadgets, (again, the dog was hiding…) Aubrey wandered into the living room.

This hallowed space doubles as my office. It is also the first room one sees upon entering our small but charming abode. So we've gussied it up with books of general interest, family photos and charming knickknacks.

Not being total dolts, we quickly stored anything that could be easily broken before the kids arrived.

The treasured miniature painting done by a renowned local artist on a stone from our one of favorite vacation spots immediately went up high. As did the two porcelain figurines made in 1965 by my wife's great grandmother. And the framed picture of my wife and me on our wedding day.

We figured the room was in pretty good shape. Silly us.

As I sat at the computer perusing the news online and checking e-mail, out of the corner of my eye I saw Aubrey opening a small wooden box. I'd completely forgotten the thing even existed, much less that it was in the room.

It had been tucked behind a stack of books, on the lower shelf of a table wedged between a chair and a corner of the wall. Not easily accessible.

But of course! We're talking about a one-year-old with hands that can magically bend and twist around corners, silently and stealthily drawing out things otherwise hidden, like a mysterious vacuum cleaner sucking invisible dust bunnies from under a bed.

Inside was a small rubber ball. And a handful of nails that I'd apparently put in there after some chore or another. And a bunch of paperclips. And a wad of notepaper. All perfectly sized for putting in her otherwise sweet, giggly, slobbery mouth.

I nearly screamed in terror!

Neon lightning flashed in my head -- nightmarish visions of having to explain to her parents how their baby had come to swallow this odd assortment of desk drawer debris.

Luckily, the baby soon tired and we put her down for a morning snooze in her port-a-crib, in our eldest daughter's room.

We were finally safe. All we had to do now was make

sure that the crib was properly locked (check) and that the sheet was correctly fitted to the mattress (check and check).

Or so I thought, until my wife instructed me to make sure the crib wasn't within an arm's length of anything in the room. The baby, my wife explained, could stand up and reach something that could be bad for her. Like the pencils off of our daughter's desk.

Yipes! Who thinks of these things? Well, babies, that's who.

This week, my wife and I will celebrate the 23rd anniversary of our first date. We will be married 19 years this September. Our children are young women, focusing on high school and college and boys (not necessarily in that order). I am getting grayer and fatter and slower by the hour. Each morning my body records more aches and pains than a doctor's diary.

But nothing in recent memory has made me feel as old as one morning with Aubrey.

Stuck on Family

I have a dilapidated old sweatshirt that is covered with glue.

After countless washings, the yellow-ish gunk remains a part of the garment, probably cooked into the material. In my frugality, I've never thrown it away. Why pitch a perfectly good sweatshirt as long as it still fits and doesn't expose my belly-button to winter's nip?

Now I am doubly glad I kept that poor excuse for clothing.

See, the glue stains are remnants of several nights of work with Al, a dear friend of mine, when we teamed up to install rubberized baseboard at our church.

As I recall, I got covered in the stuff. Al, being the more veteran installer (both in age and experience) didn't get nearly as messy. But my hands were covered in glue, a sweatshirt was handy, so a sweatshirt was used.

Al died recently.

Sitting at his memorial service, I was struck by how many people in the packed house were from our church. At least a third of the attendees were friends and acquaintances, not blood relations of Al's.

That is a much-deserved testament to Al, who was a wonderful man, always gracious, ready with a handshake and a smile.

But it also was a fascinating, fulfilling and to a degree, somewhat frightening confirmation of an apparent new phenomenon -- the idea that "family" reaches much further than our bloodlines.

Former Vice President Al Gore was on David Letterman's show recently. He and his wife, Tipper, have written a new book in which they suggest that for the first time in our cultural history, "family" is defined more by the experience of relationship, than by the actual relationship itself.

That is to say, the traditional structure of a "family" -- husband and wife and their mutual offspring -- has been replaced by the feeling of family -- we're friends, we love each other, we have important things in common, therefore we're "family."

As I suggested, this is fascinating, fulfilling and frightening all at the same time.

Fascinating and frightening, certainly as a study of and reflection on where our society is at this time in history.

The divorce rate continues to hover around 60 percent. The need for multiple incomes in many if not most American families means that our children are often cared for by an assortment of relatives, friends, neighbors and professionals.

Single parenthood comes into play as does myriad other living situations which, though a regular part of our social structure now, certainly go against what has been traditionally considered the "family" grain.

But it is also fulfilling. As I sat at Al's memorial service, sharing joys and sorrows with people I knew and didn't know, the thought occurred that in some wonderful way, through this man with whom I shared only a handful of mutual experiences, I was sitting with family.

I could not name most of the people attending that service, sharing communion regardless of our religions, listening to stories about Al told by his three children. Other than those young people and his beautiful wife, I had no connection with anyone there who does not also attend my church.

Yet sitting next to one of my best friends, Paul Spencer, whom I deeply respect and admire, whose family has become an extension of my own, I had a strong "A-ha!" moment. I realized that the former vice president was correct. We were all of us, related through our experiences with, our love for this one person.

As I said, this whole notion that the traditional structure of family has gone by the wayside speaks volumes about the status of our society.

The traditional family construct used to be defined and guided by a certain set of shared morals that, I guess, simply don't exist anymore. At least, not so much that they govern the way the majority of people run their lives.

On the other hand, the thread that ran through those morals was the idea that we are all valued, all loved, all worthy of each other's respect.

So to the degree that the "neo-family" continues to pull on that thread, there is something to be said for this new concept. You don't have to share blood with someone to share love with someone.

Thanks Al. For the sweatshirt, the memories and the border installation lessons. And, most of all, for family.